A Dog at My Heel

The companionship of a dog is an essential part of the pleasure

A DOG
AT MY HEEL

by

James Martin Young

Illustrations by Mary Young

LONDON
COUNTRY LIFE LIMITED
CHARLES SCRIBNER'S SONS
NEW YORK

First Published in 1951
by Country Life Limited
2–10 Tavistock Street, London, W.C.2
and in the United States of America
by Charles Scribner's Sons
597 Fifth Avenue, New York 17
Printed in Great Britain by
Jarrold & Sons Limited
The Empire Press, Norwich

FOR

HENRY BOARD

('GRANDAD')

CONTENTS

LIST OF ILLUSTRATIONS

9

FOREWORD

THE country, the whole of it, was made before the first brick of the first city. Every townsman has in him the blood of ancestors who left the land. Some cherish a longing to return. Almost all feel the need for an occasional visit.

This is the book of a family which went back. My wife, who drew the pictures, was born within the sound of Bow Bells; myself in a remote spot in Aberdeenshire. We met when I worked in Fleet Street and she in a London studio. A dozen years ago we moved, not without misgivings, to this old white farmhouse in Perthshire. At some unknown moment between then and now we became, in spirit as well as location, country folk again.

Our first book of this kind, *The Blue Bowl*, brought us many letters from readers at home and abroad who seemed to enjoy sharing the pastimes and adventures of a family doing in reality what so many do only in their dreams. Again, in drawings and words, we have tried to put on paper something of the feel of this way of living.

Being often unvisited from week's end to week's end, we have developed the habit of leaning casually on our field gate, ready with a welcome for anyone who cares to pause and laugh or wonder with us at the pleasures and amazements of year-round existence in the countryside. In that spirit what follows was put on record. All of it, if that matters, is strictly true.

COUPAR ANGUS,   JAMES MARTIN YOUNG
PERTHSHIRE, 1950.

PART ONE

A Dog at
My Heel

CHAPTER ONE

FAMILY CONCERN

I DON'T look under the bed for bogey-men. I am not a frightened person. Therefore when I began to feel troubled about Danny, my gun-dog, I had only too good a reason.

He was not in the prize-winning class, either on show-bench or at field trial. He had inches more leg than the ideal springer. His manners were good enough, and he was supremely biddable, but it was not in him to lie rigid at the sound of a shot, nor to ignore a couched rabbit when he was on the trail of a winged bird.

Still, he was my hound, and I had no wish for a better. I was fond of him. He shared my working hours, lying on the study floor and casting up an enticing glance whenever the wild geese went honking over the house or a pheasant crowed from the field hedge. His company was the making of my leisure. And he had me worried.

The problem could have been solved quite easily at no more expense than a couple of shillings. I had only to buy a length of chain and keep him fixed to one end of it, with the other end anchored to some sturdy hook. For Danny, who never willingly left my side in the daytime, began to develop a private night-life of his own. He became an incorrigible wanderer.

I remember meeting my friend Frank Benzies and remarking jocularly that he looked as if he had a hangover.

'Not much wonder,' he said. 'I had hardly a wink of sleep last night.'

Frank owns a Scottie bitch, and ruefully he explained that throughout the small hours some great monster of a black dog had prowled around his house serenading Micky with a ghostly, dismal howling.

'I only hope the brute doesn't come back tonight,' he said.

Frank is too good a friend to be treated with anything but shining honesty.

'I don't think it was a black dog, but a brown, roan and tan one,' I told him, 'and I believe I can guarantee that he won't come back.'

Danny found himself tied up the moment he had had his supper that evening, and the house called Hilltwegen was left in peace. But it was prevention, not cure. According to our scheme of living he could not be held prisoner all the time, and I knew no other answer to his romantic love for the open road under starry skies. Hence my fears. A dog that will not stay at home o' nights comes, at last, to no good end. Sooner or later I was going to lose him, and with him my one indispensable necessity for country living. The companionship of a dog is an essential part of the pleasure.

One day Danny rushed out to bark a boisterous welcome at a small blue car which came to our door, and to sniff with even more than usual interest at the trousers of the visitor. He was Mr James Brown, and I have never been more pleased to grant a request than the one he had come to make.

Mr Brown's hobby is the breeding and training of sporting dogs. We had met and shot together over the pleasant fields of East Camno Farm. With knowledgeable courtesy he had pointed out my springer's weak points, and still at the end of it left the final verdict unqualified:

'He's a good dog.'

There was no doubt about it. Danny, with all his faults, was a grand working dog, and Mr Brown had come to express his opinion in something more than a complimentary phrase. He wanted to mate my truant with his black-and-white bitch Meg, which I had often admired as I watched her, in Danny's company, nosing the pheasants from thicket and thorn.

'And if you care,' he said, 'you can have the pick of the litter.'

So did Danny of the gifted, sweet-natured blood, whose likeness was to be detected in half the mongrels in the district, get his chance of respectable immor-tality and myself the promise of consolation against the day when the inevitable must happen.

In time I had an invitation to call at Kinloch Kennels. The litter had arrived. The newcomer to our hearth and home was alive and in being. It would, to me, be very much a personal possession, and yet I could not deny the family an interest in it. We were all concerned—Mary, my wife, who would have to sweep up its dust and hair from the carpets; daughters Sally and Margaret, among whose multitude of pets the dogs always take first place; myself, hoping against hope that some miracle might preserve my wandering Danny and give me two first-class shooting dogs instead of one.

I tried to damp the daughters' excitement by arguing my claim to the sole right of making the selection.

'You have Gippy,' I reminded them. 'You have Flopsy, Mopsy, Tiny, Biddy-Wee, Blackie, Penny, Comfy . . .' I went grimly through the list of all the varied livestock they had gathered at Wester Denhead, not forgetting the assortment of caterpillars which inhabit a set of prefabricated shoe-box dwellings in the kitchen and which keep getting mixed up with the cooking. 'So I'm picking my own dog.'

Males are worth more money, but I had fixed my mind on a bitch. They are not so apt to go gallivanting. From my point of view Mr Brown had been bounteously blessed—the litter was nine, and eight of them were females. He carried them into his house, together with a new family of labradors, and set the whole lot down, squirming and squeaking, on the floor. Ecstatically, the children fell upon the fourteen scraps of dogs.

There were blue-roans and black-and-whites, and several sets of gingery eyebrows, but nothing to match Danny's unusual colouring. My fancy was for the commonplace liver-and-white, and I had the choice of four.

The girls lifted and sorted them, while I looked down at the wriggling mass and tried to seem wiser than I am. I have always believed it a very difficult thing to pick out the best of a litter of healthy puppies.

The children did not seem to think so.

'I want this one,' Sally decided, and set it apart.

'I want the one with the wee funny mark . . . oh! Sally's got it,' said Margie.

I have to admit that when I had gone over the four point by point—and dourly prejudiced against their favourite at that—I had to agree that she looked the queen of the lot. She was shiny and plump, interestingly marked, and with the promise of a fine head and muzzle. While Mary drew a sketch, I made up my mind.

'That's my dog,' I said.

Mr Brown called his wife, and asked her to put a finger on his own selection. It was the same one.

2

There was something of a mix-up in the family relationships of the young springers and the labradors. Mrs Lab's catering arrangements were too generously proportioned for her own family's comfort. They were more suitable for the bigger-mouthed spaniels, and so she had been foisted off with seven of them, while Danny's mate mothered the remaining two and the five labs. Afterwards, it was to be a small matter of pride to us to know that two of those self-same labradors found their way to His Majesty's kennels at Balmoral.

But this dam of kingly dogs, who was entrusted with the care of the puppy of our choice, was a careless lady. That night she lay on the promising youngster and smothered it. Very apologetically Mr Brown called us back, and we picked again after we had enjoyed a second meeting with the mixed brood of thirteen.

Thirteen . . .

Yes, again there was a tragedy, and once more it was our pup for whom the bell tolled. As if he feared we might not be able to believe in so much coincidence, Mr Brown had cut off and kept one small ear as proof of the death.

'There are two liver-and-white bitches left,' he said thoughtfully.

'And I'm not putting a hoodoo on either of them,' I declared. 'I'll come back when they have a bit more size.'

Not until they were six weeks old and ready to be independent of the labrador's outsize milk-bar did we visit Kinloch again. Then, having only two to consider, we were faced with a real problem. Which—oh, which? The one had a more massive head; the other a nicer geography of white and brown. The one had a grand, full chest a good three inches wide; the other, probably, a keener eye. I tossed small objects about, watching for early signs of the instinct to hunt and retrieve . . . and inwardly grew more and more uncomfortably certain that I knew very little about the art of judging puppy-flesh.

The daughters, meanwhile, had been viewing my meant-to-look-expert examination in silence.

'I simply don't know,' I said at last.

'Oh, Daddy, that one!' Margie cried, as if for her there were only one.

'Why, then? Why?'

'Can't you see?'

I looked, and I was darned if I could see.

'It has a white "Y" on its forehead. That means it was meant for us.'

It seemed as good a reason as any for ending the uncertainty—although in point of fact the pleasantly personal mark became nothing but a shapeless tuft

Nosing the pheasants from thicket and thorn

19

after a few weeks; too soon to leave a single record in either my wife's or Sally's sketch-books. We carried that one home to join the miniature menagerie, arguing on the way about what she should be called.

A gun-dog's name is a matter of some importance. You cannot afford to indulge in flights of fancy inspired by film-stars, cabinet ministers, or any jaw-cracking memories of classical mythology. One thing is paramount. The name must be short, sharp, and shoutable. So while the children held a private side-argument about what exactly was the halfway point where the pup should be lifted from one lap to the other on the return journey, we yapped names at each other as fast as we could think of them. The puppy was plainly astonished at finding itself in the midst of so much din.

'I like the sound of Judy,' said Sally, just as we reached home.

'Judy! Jooo-deee!' they shouted, testing it.

They have been shouting it ever since.

Gippy, the children's aged golden cocker, had just parted with her latest litter. The last pup had been spirited away an hour or two before we brought Judy home, and we had a faint hope that if it so pleased the old girl's curious mind she might be persuaded to offer what was left of her milk to the new arrival.

We set Judy down on the kitchen floor beside her, expecting nothing more than a dark look which would say as clearly as words: 'What d'you take me for?' Danny slid out of his chair and came mincing tentatively forward, stretching his neck to the fullest so that he could investigate with his nose and yet not imperil the rest of his body. Like men with small babies, male dogs always seem terrified of very young puppies.

Gippy growled horribly. I made to snatch my new possession away. But with a bark and a snap of her jaws Gippy made it quite clear that it was not the babe she was objecting to. She was telling the father of Judy and of most of her own children that things of this sort were not his business. She was inviting him, most impolitely, to hop it, and he retreated at once to his corner. Then she rolled on her side, and offered the entire freedom of the restaurant to Judy.

But if that astonished us, so did what followed. Judy had come straight from being wet-nursed by the mother of royal dogs. She would have none of Gippy's common stuff. Even when the teats were encouragingly damped with milk, she would only treat them as interesting playthings to be bitten, tugged, pounced upon, but by no means sucked.

Gippy endured it with a sweetness which was, for a self-centred matron like herself, nothing short of miraculous.

Thus we came by Judy. And thus for each of us, but especially for me, was something of first importance added to life in this Scottish farmhouse.

I would not hold that the noblest dog is of as much account as the meanest human being. Nor am I fanatically fond of animals of any kind, although this book will be full of them. I still like people better. No ancestress of mine was the famous little girl who burst into tears at the sight of the picture of the Christians being thrown to the lions, sobbing:

'There's one poor lion hasn't got a Christian!'

Never will I be heard crowing over the joys of my existence as compared with that of my brother, who is a banker in Glasgow, or of my many friends in London and elsewhere.

This life in the country is not everything; not by a long way. Myself, although I have backed my preference, I should as readily stroll through the acres of Harrod's as walk along the banks of any delightsome stream in any glen I know, catching a fine trout every fifty yards. As for fresh air, probably there can be too much of it. It is a primeval thing, and disturbing. It blows at walls, even the solid white walls of an ancient farmhouse, as if its function were to blow them away. It scatters the thoughts out of a man's head, demanding that its messages should be breathed. So, every day, I smoke thirty cigarettes in a study whose window is not opened the year through. A desk in Perthshire, with the Grampians on the right and the Sidlaws on the left and the fruitful earth of Strathmore all around, must be as much of a ball-and-chain as a desk in Fleet Street.

The advantage, for what it is, is all at the end of the working day, when you have only to be up and at the door and there you are—in the country, where at least one part of every man's spirit belongs. High school—five miles. Reference library—thirteen. Theatre, live music, and the nearest outposts of art and culture —thirteen, no less. And friends in every inaccessible place. Thrice happy townsman! Still, at the day's end, there it is—just at the door. To be lived in. To be enjoyed.

We enjoy it. I have no wish to be envied, with an ash stick to grasp or a gun to put under my arm, and a wife to capture some of the quaint moments with her pencil, and two girls to share whatever might be happening—and always, my shadow whether or not the sun be shining, a dog at my heel. There are other things to be pursued, in the course of a lifetime, besides game birds and beasts; other laughter and learning to be sought than that which has come our way with the creatures, on two legs or four, whose sharing of our existence in this remoteness has enriched and sweetened it.

But it might be that a breath of this same disturbing country air will smell wholesome and refreshing to the Glasgow brother and some others. So, in our simplicity, we introduce ourselves—a family with a new dog.

GREY LAG GOOSE

CHAPTER TWO

JUNIOR MISS

MOST of the creatures we keep and feed and care for are of no practical use whatever, and Wester Denhead might be a more comfortable place if some of the animal members of the family were to disappear.

But Judy, although she was assured of more than her fair share of affection, was never destined to be a passenger. She had a job to learn. It was certain that her work would in time become the supreme pleasure of her existence, but in spite of that she had to be taught that it was work, and so subject to rules and discipline.

We decided that Judy should not be packed off to school, but that she should be educated privately, with ourselves as her instructors. This meant that, like Danny, she would never reach the perfection of field-trial standard; but she ought to remain a more personal kind of dog than one professionally broken.

This expression, 'breaking a dog'—I don't like it. A few trainers still seem to act by it, and in the shooting field one meets with hounds so controlled, so subdued, that they can hardly be induced to leave their masters' feet. It is especially unpleasant to see this over-subjugation in a spaniel. The essence of the spaniel nature is bounce, vitality, busy curiosity about every piece of cover.

They are superb, indefatigable hunters, and no matter where he may be placed in the line of guns, the man who owns an active spaniel is the man who sees most game. It is a waste of their finest quality to teach them that hunting is a crime.

At the same time, there has to be some restraint. Never would I own one of those tinkers' curs that go yelping over several counties after every hare that shows itself. Never would I have my name on the collar of such a tike . . . and I hasten to add that our independent old Gippy did not wear a collar, and that in any case she was the children's, not mine.

Somehow Judy had to be divorced from the sinful delight of chasing, and I discovered a retired gamekeeper who could tell me exactly how to do it.

'Peg your dog down on a long, strong cord in some closed-in place,' he said, 'and put a rabbit or two in beside her and let them run about. Every time she sets off after one, the cord will jerk her back. She'll no' like it. She'll get it into her mind that if she doesna' bide still, she might pu' her heid off! Then you can do the same with a winged doo, or a pheasant.'

Six months is the age when a novice's training is supposed to begin, and I was quite content to wait until the spring, leaving Judy in the meanwhile with nothing to do but develop muscle and bone. The children were not so patient. They were all for making a start as soon as she had arrived.

The only enclosed place they could discover was the kitchen floor, where the old flagstones have been covered by a layer of red-tinted cement. It was out of the question to drive a peg into that, but a length of string tied to the leg of the table seemed good enough.

Sally brought in Flopsy, one of her own rabbits, and set her down beside the puppy which, having submitted to the fitting of its first collar, had gone to sleep in a cushioned kipper-box beside the range. Flopsy needed no encouragement to do her stuff. She hopped into the cosily padded box and, finding it to her liking, she nosed and pushed until she had turfed the discomfited Judy out. Meekly Judy made do with a place on the hearth rug.

Margie tried next with Blackie and Penny, the bantams—were they not as good as winged pheasants or 'doos'? She carried them indoors, one under each arm, and put them on the floor while Judy happened to be enjoying a snack. The pair of little hens marched straight to her dish, churring warningly. She retreated in astonishment before them, nor would she venture back to her meal until they had satisfied themselves and flown up to warm their feet on top of the electric cooker.

I began to wonder if I shouldn't have to reverse the usual process, and find some way of training a bit of devil into my new dog.

Then there was the technique of retrieving. Judy was only eleven weeks old when I was boasting to my 'keeper friend:

'The children have her carrying an empty cartridge and a golf ball already.'

'Aye,' he said glumly, 'and she takes it away and chews it up, likely.'

'Not her! Believe me, she brings it to hand.'

After all, that had been true—once or twice.

'You'll spoil your bitch,' he insisted, 'unless you learn her once an' for all to be saft in the moo. It's as well to start right.'

I had uneasy memories of pheasants I have plucked, carried by other men's dogs, their breasts pitted deep with fang-marks. And some of those cartridges, as well as the old golf ball, had finished by being chewed.

'Have you a tip, then,' I asked, 'for keeping a dog soft in the mouth?'

'A hedgehog!'

'What . . .'

'An old one. They have sharper spikes.'

'How . . .?'

'Put it inside a rabbit's skin, and sew it up. Learn her to fetch that. So long as she's saft in the moo she'll come to no harm. But she'll soon see what she gets if she grips!'

He had a gleam in his eye, the old gamie. He was one who always spoke about 'breaking' a dog.

I never shocked Judy with a hedgehog disguised as a rabbit. As it turned out, there was no need. With hounds, as with humans, the first secret of success in life is to choose the right parents. We spent many a happy hour on Judy's education, and we taught her quite a number of things; but we ourselves learned a few items also, and especially about the value of good breeding. The man who taught Judy to be 'saft in the moo' must have died many years before she was born, and, if anything, he did the job too well. She is so gentle with game that she is almost sloppy in her carrying.

It was an enchanting pastime, persuading her to go chasing after things rolled or thrown, and always, unfailingly, to yield them up to hand—never, never to drop them on the ground. A shooting man can look mighty silly when his retriever sets a lightly shot bird down at his feet, and it takes wing and flies back to the covert.

The children's enthusiasm never flagged, and they were unbending in their insistence on: 'To hand! Bring it to hand!' Their methods may have been unorthodox, but they worked on sound enough principles, as on the day when it crossed their minds that it would be fun to teach Judy to go for her dish when she wanted a tit-bit.

'Fetch your dish, Judy! Fetch your dish!' I heard it from the kitchen not once but a hundred times, until I had to cry for mercy. I couldn't stand it.

'She's only a pup, you know,' I reminded them. 'She has no idea of what you're saying.'

Later the same day I entered the kitchen, to be half-deafened by a sudden chorus of: 'Fetch your dish! Fetch your dish!'

Judy stirred in her sleeping box, and gave a small grunt, and made to settle again. But they kept on shouting at her, and at last, genial soul that she always was, she scrambled to the floor. I stared at her, amazed. She was fat to bursting point; so fat that she could scarcely walk, but only waddle. She reached her dish and picked it up.

'To hand, now! To hand!'

She carried it to Sally's hand, and was rewarded with a couple of biscuits from a bag that had shrunk in proportion to Judy's increase in girth. She had learned that trick in one easy lesson, and it has never been forgotten. She still goes and fetches her dish without any command whenever she feels like a little something—and it can be awkward, when the dish happens to be filled with some mess that has not taken her fancy. Then, one meal is apt to be scattered greasily over the floor while she comes cadging for another.

We waited with some anxiety for Judy's first introduction to gunfire. More than once I have seen a promising young dog turn about and go slinking off at the sound of a shot. Some can be cured of it, gradually. Some remain gunshy, and for the good of the breed it might be better to have them destroyed. They are often seen advertised: 'cheap to good home'. They are likely to have other faults, and can turn out to be bad bargains.

Judy was three months old, and at that too young by half, when she had her first business outing. Of course, she had Danny for company.

All the books declare that nothing helps so much in the education of a youngster as to watch a wise adult dog at work. I suppose it is true; but certainly not in the case of a pup so small and airy-minded as Judy was then. She spent most of the time leaping at Danny's flapping ears and doing her best to have them off. As he was quite unable to work with any style, Judy could learn nothing from him that day—unless it was a magnificent lesson in patience and forbearance.

A rabbit got up. I fired. It rolled over. Danny dashed to get it, while I watched the pup. At the sudden bang, although I had made up my mind not to expect such perfection from her, she had come to heel and was sitting at my feet. But she had not come in fear. Not Judy! Head on one side, eyes popping, she was looking on as her sire retrieved, and quite plainly the blood of all her ancestors, leaping and exultant, was shouting within her:

'This is life!'

Each time the trigger was pulled that afternoon Judy squatted at heel as smartly as if she had been professionally broken. When next I met the old 'keeper I was keen to tell him about the try-out.

'Too young! Too young, man,' he said, before I had got well started. 'I ken fine what happened. At every shot she was away across the countryside, barkin' like mad.'

'The devil she wasn't!'

'But there's a cure for it,' he told me. 'Take the shot but not the powder out of a cartridge, and re-load it with wheat. When your bitch runs in—let her have it in the behind! She'll no' need many doses. It nips, but it does no damage. If a grain or two sticks in her hide, you can pike them out with the point o' your knife.'

I know some other characters who might be none the worse for a charge of wheat in the behind—and I don't mean dogs.

A month later, somewhere among the wires of the raspberry fields around Wester Denhead, Danny broke a toe. Happily the children fell to the task of nursing him, fixing the injured limb up with splint and bandage and several yards of sticking plaster. Putting on a doleful face, he posed in his chair for a portrait, or went stumping about the house holding up the dressed paw and asking for sympathy. No human ever relished a minor hurt more than a petted dog can. Meanwhile, in the pleasantest part of the shooting season, I was without a nose.

'Give Gippy a chance! You never do,' Sally pleaded.

Wild, lawless, self-willed Gippy had had her last chance, so far as I was concerned, on the afternoon when she went barging down a ditch and put out no fewer than fifteen pheasants at ranges up to three hundred yards. Besides, she was already suffering from the complaint which was soon to end her life.

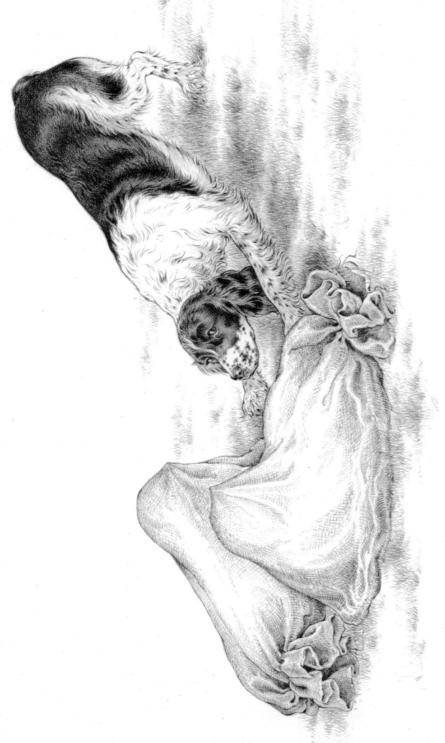

Nothing can ever happen but a dog must have a share in it

'Why not Judy?' said Margie.

'For one thing, it's only four months since she was born. What use d'you think she'd be at that age? I haven't even begun to train her yet.'

But the raspberry fields where I was privileged to shoot were a paradise of game while the leaf was still on the canes. They talked me into it.

In the centre of one of the plantations I had a long shot at a covey of partridges, and dropped one in what was, for any dog, a veritable jungle of cover. I made my way over the wires to the spot where I thought it had fallen, and encouraged Judy to sniff around. She showed no interest. She wanted to go scampering off in quite another direction.

Finally, very disgruntled, and narking irritably at my feather-brained pup, I emptied the gun and turned for home. It was worse than useless, killing birds and allowing them to lie and rot.

For a moment I did not notice that Judy had slipped out of sight. Sharply I called her back—she must not learn to go careering through the rasp drills hunting for her own pleasure. From an archway of canes on the line which she had been so eager to take all the time the plump figure came pushing out, a flapping partridge secure in her baby jaws. She brought it smartly to hand. She gave it up without fuss or ceremony, and stood cheerfully watching for the next move.

A very small event, I suppose, to be catalogued as one of the absolutely perfect moments of a man's life.

The presence in the home of a charming and gifted young daughter, whose company he obviously loved, did nothing to make my old rascal of a Danny mend his ways. As soon as his toe had healed he went a-roving again.

Walking the fields, or sitting with me by the river waiting for the dusk flight of the wildfowl, he would lift his head and, nostrils quivering, sense news in the air. He was too much of a gentleman ever to slip off and leave me high and dry. But forthwith he would jot down a compass bearing in his mental engagement diary.

He was a dog who liked his food. He always ate hugely, and he preferred to be well fortified inwardly before he set off to answer the invitation borne on the wind. After a hearty supper a dog needs a moment to nip out and wash his hands—and when Danny had an appointment, that was his time.

He would never disobey me directly. If I were there and called him in, he would come. Well did he know how I disapproved of his amorous excursions, but again and again he managed to make an exit unnoticed, and I was lenient, doing little more than grumbling at him and hoping for the best. It was quite a different kettle of fish when he began to take his innocent young daughter away.

'Take' might be unfair to him. I dare say he would have been only too glad to shake her off, if he could have done it. But she had a boundless affection for him, and letting them out one at a time for the handwashing was no answer. Judy had her father's nose—and darkness hides no secrets in the canine world.

I have often wondered what happened when she caught up with him, away in the shadowy lanes. Did he try to pack the little minx off home? He certainly could not have wanted her trailing him, but from what I know of him he was too good-humoured by half to turn upon her with a snarl or a showing of his teeth.

Quite sharply did Danny learn, after the first time, that whether he had enticed her or not, leading Judy astray was crime in the first degree. Both had a lesson after the second time, for instead of slinking into the kitchen in the morning, bespattered with mud and guilt, they chose to creep secretively into the shed where, among other things, upward of five hundred garden canes are kept. What happened was meant in all sincerity for their own good.

Yet I have to confess that I have never known the stick to teach any dog anything except how to look cowed. What they cannot learn by word and gesture and common understanding will never be whacked into them, and although I was born in a part of Scotland where soft-heartedness is almost the chief of the seven deadly sins, I have never whacked Judy since that morning, nor ever had reason to think she is a worse dog for want of it.

They did stay at home for a short time afterwards, but probably only because Danny had no engagements. Soon the call came to him again, and again at dusk he vanished and Judy followed.

Danny's custom, always, was to make a night of it, and his reappearance around breakfast-time was masterly in its inconspicuousness. I scarcely ever saw him come. One minute his chair would be empty; the next, there he was, silent, shrunk into himself, uneasily awaiting the volley of sharp words which he heard with so much unhappiness. So I was astonished when, on that particular night, I heard the scrape of a rough pad on the back door at ten o'clock. Odd! It was the first time he had advertised himself in such a way.

Angrily I marched to let him in, while a voice called after me:

'Oh, Jimmie, don't be hard on him! It's good of him, bringing Judy back.'

'He shouldn't have taken her away,' said I. But I let my walking-stick stand in its corner.

He dodged past me and into his chair while I waited to say a piece to the youngster. There was no sign of her. I searched in all the corners where she might be hiding and thinking belatedly of those five hundred canes. She was nowhere.

Back in the kitchen I found Danny with a different look. He was not crouching guiltily trying to make himself seem as small as possible, but sitting up and giving out small, miserable, whining sounds, as if there were some intolerable burden on his mind.

'Where's Judy?' I asked him. 'Where's Judy?'

I was fairly sure that he was doing his best to tell me that something had happened to the little one. I found myself remembering many a tale of shepherds' dogs leading their masters over hill and dale to the one lost sheep; all kinds of hounds leading all kinds of people to storm-stayed travellers and what-not. No doubt every one of those tales was true. Certain breeds have remarkable powers in that direction. But not spaniels. Clever as they are, such feats are not in their repertoire. Although Danny evidently knew where Judy was, or could easily have put his nose to the ground and followed the trail, force of habit was too much for him. Out of doors he merely came to heel with that excessive anxiety to be mannerly which he always showed when he had a guilty conscience. He waited as usual for me to be the guide. The night was pitch-black, and I had no idea which way to turn in the circle of the surrounding countryside.

I have a parlour trick which my children are apt to mention at awkward moments. More than once, at a lull in the conversation with some visitor, a young voice has piped up:

'Daddy, wiggle your ears!'

I remember how it started—on a day when a dreary teacher was struggling to pump the elements of Latin into a class of still drearier thirteen-year-olds. Bored, I tried to feel the muscles that move the ears. I discovered them. It was a rare sensation; as if a new part of me had come to birth. I have used them ever since, and recommend everyone else to try to do likewise. Whenever I want very specially to pick up some faint sound, up go my ears like a donkey's, tensed and wide, and it certainly improves the hearing.

So I sent Danny home with his scufflings and scrapings, and moved in this direction and that, cocking my ears and listening.

There is no such thing as silence in the countryside. Curlews and peewits; wild-duck wings and bleating sheep; the squealing of a snared rabbit; the stir

3

of life in the very earth itself—always, there is some sound. I kept calling and waiting for an answer, and after two hours I heard it—a tiny, pitiful yelping from very far away. I followed it for a good mile across the fields, and found Judy with one leg caught fast in the steel jaws of a gin-trap.

The bone was not broken. She was more frightened than hurt. If I had not come upon her she would have survived the night, and I have no reason to think that in the morning the trapper, whoever he was, would have done other than set her free, and give her a friendly pat, and send her home.

At the same time, I can never forget my Aunt Mary's fur rug. It was a beautiful, soft, cosy rug that draped the end of her sofa, and in my boyhood I used to love to press my face against it and work my fingers through the silky, springy hair. I coveted it. I wished my people had one just like it. Yet such a one could not be bought. It was unique among all the rugs I have ever seen. There were snowy-white sections in it, and sable, and grey, and ginger, and rectangles interestingly patterned in tortoiseshell. It was made of the skins of cats that had gone prowling by night, and every one of them had done exactly what Judy had done, and blundered into a rabbit trap.

Judy's pretty brown and white would have looked quite as handsome in a rug as any cat's pelt—and men whose business it is to set traps have no special reason to feel generously disposed towards unwanted beasts which get caught in them.

Something had to be done.

WOOD-PIGEONS

CHAPTER THREE

DAY OF RECKONING

THERE were three ways of putting an end to Danny's misbehaviour. I had to sell him, shoot him, or chain him.

If his sin had been sheep-worrying, there would not have been three but only one. But whatever else he got up to on his midnight meanderings, I was perfectly certain that he took no notice of the sheep. In hunting, nothing bigger than a hare or a wild goose held any interest for him, as he proved on the one and only occasion when I fired both barrels of a twelve-bore at a roe deer. It was so badly wounded that it could only just keep ahead of me as I followed it up over heather and bog-myrtle, and no amount of exhortation would persuade Danny to go after it and stop it, as he could so easily have done.

The stricken deer vanished at last into a half-mile-square wood of dense young fir, and I lost it. It has been on my conscience ever since. I'll never do the like again, and I think it might make for the peace of mind of other sportsmen if they decided to keep their barrels down when such a chance presents itself and they are carrying small shot. It might have been better to have aimed for the heart instead of the head, but that is a point which I'll not put to the test.

Danny had years of usefulness left in him, and as between putting him down and finding a new home for him there seemed to be no argument. Far too many valuable dogs are slaughtered every year because their owners feel they would be unhappy among strangers. What rubbish! It is true enough that a dog's homing instinct will often take him over incredible distances back to his old abode, but keep him leashed for a time and let him get acquainted, and he will soon be as firmly attached to the new master as the old.

So, one day when I was among a party of shooting men, I drew in a sharp breath and said in passing:

'I'm thinking of selling Danny.'

That was all. I did not offer him for sale, nor even say that he was definitely on the market. Simply: 'I'm thinking . . .'

It was a bleak thought, too; and not less so because around that time our old character of a Gippy, too ill to find any more fun in life, had vanished from Wester Denhead on a day when I got all the rest of the family away from home.

The next afternoon, when I came back from a visit to Dundee to the greeting of two dogs instead of three, I could see at a glance that something was wrong. The children, who had accepted Gippy's passing as an inevitable thing, rushed at me in accusation.

'Daddy, you can't do it! You couldn't!'

'Do what?' I said.

'Sell Danny.'

'Who said I was going to sell him?'

There had been a caller in my absence. His card was on the brass tray. He had heard that Danny was on the market, and despite all the protests I rang him up. He offered me a very handsome price. Moreover—and of course it was a consideration—he had an ideal place for a dog. Danny would have to live in a kennel, but in the company of others of his kind. I knew that this man would have cherished my wandering tike and been good to him. But:

'Daddy—you couldn't!'

And whether or not I could, I didn't. And not entirely because it would have upset the children, either.

So I invested a florin, and fixed up a hook by the old wicker chair in the corner of the kitchen. From that time onwards it was the stern rule of the household that never, repeat never, unless I their master took them abroad, were both Danny and Judy to be free at one and the same time. One or other of them must be on that chain throughout the day.

'Or Danny goes,' I said.

It was a most vexing and uncomfortable arrangement.

In one respect, Danny was a case for a psycho-analyst. It would have been interesting to get at the root cause of his claustrophobia.

I have written about it in my book *The Blue Bowl*—how he could not bear to be left alone in a room, but must always have one of his people within sight of him. His chair was a cosy enough spot for any dog. There was always a fire in the kitchen range, and always someone popping out and in with a friendly word for him. So long as he had company he endured his lion's share of the imprisonment quite patiently, but whenever he was left by himself, even for a few minutes, he set up a miserable crying that echoed through the house and upset everyone. Judy, when it was her turn, would yelp indignantly for a time and then curl up and go to sleep. My tough old sinner of a Danny behaved like a baby.

Often, at Judy's expense, we were forced to unfasten him and put the daughter on the chain instead. A number of times he vanished in spite of all our watch-fulness; especially when I myself was from home. One day, to the delight of the children, he turned up in one of the classrooms at the local school. Another time—and for this we never found any explanation—he came home with the milk out of a night of storm, his fur plastered all over with a thick dough of wet flour, almost enough to make a four-pound loaf.

'I'll simply have to get rid of him,' I kept saying, and never did, and knew that my own weakness was certain to cost him and me its price sooner or later. Knowing, I threw out a hint that I had a birthday coming off shortly, and that a portrait of Danny in water-colours would look well on the wall above my study desk.

The rumour that he was for sale got about, and I had half a dozen offers for him. I was made to feel that I might as well put the baby up for sale. He was one of the family; possessed not only by ourselves but also by our neighbours.

He was indiscriminately fond of the entire human race, and if a burglar had broken into our house it is pretty certain that Danny would have licked his hand. The only people with whom he was deservedly unpopular were some other dog-owners. Danny's harem, in his own opinion, included every bitch within a circuit of three miles. Any other male hound on his territory was a rival to be tackled and summarily destroyed. Many a time I have been embarrassed as he set upon some sedate brother taking a stroll inoffensively at the end of a lead.

In every other way he was gentle. If he came in, as he often did, to find old Blackie the bantam occupying his chair, it would never have crossed his mind to turn her out. He would let the white mice crawl over him, the tame rabbits nestle against him by the fireside, the canary perch on his head. The children could sit on him, stand on him, ride on his back, do anything with him.

There was a discussion some time ago in the correspondence columns of a literary journal about the stupidity of illustrating junior books with pictures of animals ridiculously dressed up. Young people, most of the writers declared, were far more interested in animals as they really are. I was almost tempted to break the rule imposed upon me by my first chief reporter in the worthy city of Aberdeen: 'Never write anything you're not to be paid for!' I wanted to agree with the majority opinion—and then to tell about the day when some shooting friends called for me, and I whistled for my dog, and he came hobbling out attired in a pink jumper, a red-spotted skirt, two pairs of juvenile shoes, and with blue ribbons decorating his ears.

Danny was pampered and spoiled, and yet still a superb gun-dog. All the indulgences he received failed to make him soft. He was tough and courageous and wise—oh, wise to the ways of game, and often sharper witted than I. That winter, well knowing he was in disgrace as he took turns with Judy on the chain, he reacted as dogs will. They bear no resentment. They do not go into the sulks. They have an infinite capacity for forgiving, and are as ready to come offering an apology whether they be in the right or in the wrong. Danny and I were the better friends because of his punishment. That season was probably the best we ever had.

It was the last.

It might have been that in his wisdom Danny knew that above all other game I cherished the greylag goose. Down by the Isla river, in the freezing dusk or dawn, he would wait and listen beside me, and when the call of the flighting geese sounded he would tense and tremble with excitement, as eager as I that this time, this time, they might choose to fly over our heads.

Danny and I made our final visit to the river on a perishingly cold dawn in January. We heard the greylags. We saw them come out of the darkness, and by a miracle they headed straight towards us. As they passed over I hesitated about firing, for they were very high, but I gave the leading bird the choke barrel with a special loading of BB. It rocked and then picked itself up and flew on strongly with the others.

We heard the greylags. We saw them come out of the darkness

Danny was determined to be after them. I could hardly hold him back. Daylight came up without the offer of another shot, and still, as I turned for home, Danny insisted that he wanted to be away in the direction the flock had taken.

From the top of the river's flood-bank I could see them in a grass field nearly a mile up-river, and although I told myself that there was no hope, a wild-fowler must always be hopeful. Besides, I had learned to have a healthy respect for Danny's intelligence.

I parked bag and gun—I had no shooting rights over this ground—and I went trudging towards the geese, thinking there might be a thousand-to-one chance that when they rose, the pricked one would remain. When we were near enough I sent Danny amongst them, and they got up with a thousand-tongued flurry of abuse at being disturbed just as they were starting breakfast. But all of them flew off. The odd one did not stay.

My own breakfast was overdue. Danny never had any, so he had no reason to hurry. Back we turned—and halfway to the parked bag and gun Danny stopped and gave an interested 'Wuff!' He was staring across a hard-frozen ploughed field.

'Wuff!'

I looked. All that was to be seen there was a couple of crows sitting dismally on the sterile furrows, shoulders hunched.

'Silly old devil!' I said. 'What's taken you? We're not reduced to crow pie yet!'

He knew as well as I did the difference between game birds and non-game birds, except that throughout his lifetime he never lost his habit of pouncing upon water-hens and bringing them to me. But as we marched on he kept stopping and staring at the brace of crows fluffed there on the empty land, and at last his interest in them made me ask myself—what were they doing there? What comfort and joy was there for a pair of crows on iron-hard plough on a snell January morning? Why weren't they, too, off to breakfast?

'All right, old boy,' I said. 'If you're looking for exercise before you go back on the chain, you can investigate.'

The two black devils took wing as soon as he entered the field. He gave them only a passing glance and held on. From a furrow close by where they had been waiting, my greylag got up and flew, but could not rise more than a few feet from the ground. Danny overtook him; leapt and caught him on the wing; head-high carried him back, all eight pounds of him; and whether he deserved it or not I gave him credit for working out, minutes sooner than I did, the reason why two carrion crows had seemed to have had no thought about breakfast.

There is a very well-known news-photograph, taken years ago in the East End of London, which shows a bulldog-jawed figure pressed protectively into a shabby doorway but thrusting out a curious and aggressive face as he takes a peek at something off-stage and obviously dangerous. Behind this central character are three police officers, hugging the wall.

The scene is Sidney Street, on the day of the famous siege, when the notorious Peter the Painter, cornered, was putting up his last fight. And if Peter had taken a pot at that group and bagged a couple of them, Britain would have had to look elsewhere for a wartime Prime Minister, and I in some other quarter for a father-in-law. One of those bobbies survived to be my children's well-loved Grandad.

He left his native Devon to pass his working life as a detective in London, and as soon as he had finished the job the country called him and he hastened back to the west. He is a frequent visitor at Wester Denhead, and it was doubly pleasant on that morning of the crows to carry home a goose and have him share the whole incident to its last minutest detail, with special emphasis on Danny's astuteness.

In a hundred ways this latest visit of my father-in-law made life at Wester Denhead pleasanter, and not the least was the ending of the constant, mournful howling that had kept breaking out whenever Danny was left alone. Danny was never alone while Grandad was with us. The two were old acquaintances and bosom friends. In past seasons they had spent hours together by the chilly river, and Grandad was always more generous than I in the way of patting and petting.

He and Danny had certain private arrangements which were supposed to be secret from me; especially in the dining-room. I never give my dogs tit-bits at table. Never, never, never. Too often have I sat in other people's houses and been pestered by greedy beggars pawing and whimpering and talking out of turn. My springer knew the law, and so did my relations—but I was aware of what happened many a time when Danny cast a furtive glance at me, and slid under the table!

Grandad loved Danny; quite enough, on the evening after the greylag was found, when my wife and I were out and the children in bed, to give up his chair in the lounge and go and sit in the kitchen with the prisoner.

My father-in-law's professional life had been spent in dealing with criminals, and like most wise-minded police officers, he took a very human view of them. In all the fascinating reminiscences he has recounted in my presence, I have never heard him describe any crook as absolutely evil. He has often spoken with pity about people he has had to arrest.

He pitied Danny—and Danny knew it. We were scarcely out of the house when a sad, small whimper came from the wicker chair, and of course there was no harm whatever in unfastening the convict and letting him have the freedom of the kitchen.

Judy, as well as Danny, was delighted. She bounded at her sire, and the two played a rough-and-tumble game on the floor, rolling and snarling and struggling over an old slipper. It was a curious thing that although the pair would play like that by the hour under the eyes of any other member of the family, Danny always cut the frolic short when I came in. He seemed to feel the need for due dignity in the company of his master.

They played—and then, in time, both went to the door and looked round appealingly. But the man who had taken a part in the siege of Sidney Street was not that kind of a softie.

'Oh, no you don't!' he said, and let Judy out alone, and then secured her on the chain while he personally escorted Danny into the darkness. Danny disappeared round the end of the house.

He did not come back.

It was a thing that had happened to myself dozens of times, and the news did not startle me when we arrived home at midnight.

'Let's lock the door and forget it,' I said. 'He'll turn up. He always does.'

In the morning we had a call from one of the hardy band of women who work at all seasons in the raspberry fields. She looked distressed. Tears came to her eyes.

'Oh, Mr. Young, I don't know how to tell you!'

'Not . . . Danny?' I said. I was well prepared. I had been expecting it for two years.

'Yes, it's him. There's been an accident.'

'Killed?' I said.

'He's dead. Lying at the side of the road just up by Sandy Ritchie's.'

I was grateful to her for her tender feelings. Danny had known the raspberry workers well; known too, to a minute, the hour of their mid-morning snack, when they always had something for him.

With some deliberation I took breakfast, while the children cried, and Mary carried a tray to Grandad's bedroom and made an evasive answer when he asked who had come knocking so early. When I had finished my meal I went and dug a sizeable hole at the edge of our two-acre field, somewhere near the flowering currant bush. I trundled the wheelbarrow up to the bend by the corner of Ritchie's Lane.

There was Danny, with a gruff old countryman of my acquaintance trumpet-ing into a coloured handkerchief as he stood looking down at the corpse.

'Must ha' been a lorry,' he said.

'I expect so.'

'He wasn't a bad dog.'

'Not bad,' I said.

'A bit long in the leg, but . . . man, it's a pity.'

'Can't be helped,' I said.

'The lorry driver might ha' stopped.'

'Wouldn't have done much good if he had, would it?'

I bore no grudge against the driver who had not stopped. It was no fault of his. Doubtless he had done his best to swerve as the dark shape streaked across his path in the grey dawn, and he had probably risked his neck. The guilt was mine for having a dog wandering on the road at a dangerous bend. Nor did I feel any grudge against Grandad for what he had done, except that I wished fervently that my hand and not his had opened the door on the fatal night.

Danny had asked for it, time and again. Now he had got it. I could not help experiencing a dark satisfaction at the thoroughness of the job. He had certainly never felt it. I picked up his heart ten yards from his body.

There was no ceremony over his funeral. I buried him in the hole I had dug, and that was that. Many animal graves are dotted about Wester Denhead, but this one alone bears no wooden cross, no primrose plant, no rectangle of white stones, nothing. Life is for the living. I do not believe in mourning for dead men, let alone dead dogs. But soft-hearted or not, I had been very fond of Danny.

His picture, painted to the life by Mary, hangs above my desk. Every hair is true. I feel I could reach up and give a tug at the curly, brown ear. I have only to glance at the ginger muzzle to remember a thousand pleasant moments out in the countryside. I glance at it most days, thinking back—and thanking my stars for Mr Brown, and for Judy.

PARTRIDGES

CHAPTER FOUR

LIVING AND LEARNING

WHEN my car goes wrong, I don't tinker with it myself but send an SOS to Mr Lamb. So, too, with watch or plumbing or any other bit of mechanism that needs attention—it pays in the long run to call in an expert.

But a gun-dog need not be merely a machine. It can be an extension of its owner's self. Much, much more can be got from it than the putting up and retrieving of game.

The man who wants nothing from his spaniel but robot efficiency should entrust its training to some competent gamekeeper, whose fee will add up to only a penny or two per hour for all the work he will put in. I have not a word to say against the good professional trainer, who does very well indeed what often amounts to little more than a labour of love. But the man who enjoys his dog's society, and who gets at least half his shooting pleasure from watching and controlling it, is missing something if he lives out his whole life without trying his damnedest to do at least once what I did with this Judy of mine. He should train a dog for himself. Like me, he will most likely make a poorish job of it, and for years afterwards will be irritated by the faults he has failed to correct. But he will be amply rewarded in other ways.

It is not nearly so complicated as the books make it sound. Given a puppy with the right blood, half the work will have been done before it is begun. The

46

rest, it seems to me, depends on just how much one is entitled to expect from a dog, and just how resolutely one keeps insisting on certain rules.

For instance, no man of sense would let his children go barging into the dining-room ahead of his guests and himself, and in the same way he should look to his dog to sit at fences and wait until he is through and his gun re-loaded. If the puppy is always called back, and always made to sit, that piece of politeness soon becomes second nature.

Then there is this business of being steady. It is what a man wants most of all—a steady dog; not a mute, over-disciplined paragon that slogs along at heel by the hour taking no interest in anything whatsoever, nor a beast that leaps into every thicket without a by-your-leave and is soon heard yelping its head off a couple of hundred yards away, but an animal that can be trusted either in the open or in cover to keep contact with his owner and show a little self-restraint.

With Danny gone, I had to make do without the influence of the older dog in Judy's training, and I worked to an utterly simple principle which, as it turned out, served excellently. In essence it was the same technique as I or anyone would employ in writing a book, or setting out a bed of dahlias, or carving some nick-nack from a piece of wood. The secret, I think, is to start with a clear vision of the finished job. There, in your pipe-dreams, is perfection—and a lifetime of the disappointments of creative work must never teach you that in the end perfection is always unattainable. You slog away, ever hopeful and ever dissatisfied, with as strong a will as you may possess, adding and discarding, developing and checking, until you feel your capacity is exhausted and you shrug and decide to make do.

I asked myself what sort of dog I wanted Judy to be, and realized as I thought it over that the answer was comfortably modified. I will say nothing about my books, but my bits of wood-carving are never meant for the Royal Academy, nor my dahlia beds for the eyes of the Director of Kew Gardens. Equally, a pottering shooter's spaniel can be considerably less than a field-trial champion, nor must it necessarily be schooled to the same hard pattern as a professional trainer's pupil, which has to be so educated that its conduct will find acceptance with any stranger who might want to buy it.

All I desired was a useful kind of beast, zestful but biddable, enterprising but controlled, which would find and put up any game which happened to lie within gunshot of my line of walk, and retrieve what was killed without disturbing the ground ahead.

That was the outline of the picture, and whether wisely or not, I decided to waste no time in cultivating a set of those artificial tricks which are so dear to some dog-breakers, and so impressive to unwary buyers. I had no interest in a hound which would sit rock-still while I flung my bonnet over the hedge, and wait until I counted ten, and then at a signal spring to recover it. Birds and beasts, not bonnets, were to be Judy's business. The children's efforts in that line were quite enough for me. It seemed more practical to go straight to the field.

This finding and raising of the quarry is no mean task. Every man who has ever carried a gun knows how close game will lie. There can be no shooting company which has not noticed how regularly something gets up just at that moment when there is a pause to light a cigarette and discuss the next move—and the dogs have been left free to sniff around.

The spaniel, therefore, must learn to work the ground, and to make a success of that he must not be thinking all the time that he is venturing where he ought not to be; neither must he imagine that this is his picnic, and that his master has only brought him out to enjoy a carefree romp.

His place is anywhere and everywhere within a twenty-yard semicircle ahead. That is his territory. He has the full freedom of it, except in those places where it is better to keep him at heel. If the dog's own pleasure in the day's outing be a consideration to the man with the gun—and indeed it generally is—then let him discover that there are delights enough for any one moment in this strictly limited area. Let his joy, and his duty, be to spot every living thing inside it, and chase it out—but not away over the horizon!

In other words, the ideal is to have him constantly active, vitally interested, but fixed by an invisible twenty-yard cord to his master's cartridge belt.

Besides the novice dog's natural urge to go racing straight ahead, various distractions tend to snap that cord. There is your wise old rabbit or hare that lies doggo to the last second, well knowing how much better it is to be passed by than to make a run for it with shot whistling about its ears. Secretly it couches until your eager pup's jaws almost snap its rump—and then off, weaving and dodging, and the dog bursting to be after it. Almost as tempting is the pheasant or the partridge covey which has heard you coming and has taken a discreet departure, leaving the ground rich with that mysterious allure which is so titillating to the canine nose.

Your pup must make that canny veteran bolt. He must notice that scent and pass on the exciting information that birds are at hand. But he must learn that such thrills are your concern as well as his own; that he is merely the junior member of a partnership—and that you, lumbering human, have only two weary legs to his tireless four.

How, then, to fix this invisible cord? There is another and a better way, I think, than by starting with a real cord and letting the pup 'near pu' his heid off' every time he makes a self-willed rush. It is based on what I consider to be the natural and proper relationship between a man and his dog.

I looked forward to spending countless pleasant leisure hours in Judy's sole company, and I knew from old experience the curiously fascinating unity which would develop between us. I should become attached to her, and she to me, in affection and understanding. But this oneness, this mutual love of man and dog, is usually expressed in terms of human associations, and they are deceiving. It is companionship of a sort, but it is both less and more. It is, as I see it, achieved in an entirely different way from any friendship between man and man. Not in any sense is it a similar thing.

I intended to dominate Judy in a way in which I could never imagine myself dominating any person. I meant to teach her that my will was her only law. I planned to do this in such a manner that she would never know fear of me, nor shame me in company by cringing away from my uplifted hand. She was to be my dog. I was to be her master. My dictatorship was to be absolute, but both of us, on the different planes of man and dog, were to like it.

The invisible cord, then, was to be made of nothing stronger than the strength of my own determination to possess, in Judy, exactly the kind of spaniel I desired.

She proved to be a very gifted and tractable little bitch. But I, alas, am not a superman.

How blessed a thing it is to have kindly neighbours! Ours are of the best, and one of them, a lady far into her nineties, used to declare in her last bed-ridden years that she loved to hear me banging around with my gun.

Mrs Ferguson gave me, among other things, the freedom of a twenty-acre field of old grass where, through the summer, a couple of coveys of partridges often lay, and where, on a sunny afternoon, there were always sure to be a few baby rabbits and the odd old buck or doe lying in the long tussocks. That field was Judy's school. The pair of us walked it together until we knew every blade of grass in it. Time and again we disturbed the partridges at their afternoon nap, and Judy knew them from the days when they were only cheepers blundering off on foot while the parent birds fluttered and protested a yard or two from her excited nose. She saw them take their first rocky little flights; she saw them grow until they were able to go churring off, flinging back derisive chatter.

Dearly would she have liked to go dashing among the helpless chicks and gather up a mouthful of them. But from the first she was made to understand that, however delicious the scent might be, her part was like that of the Bisto kids on the poster. She might sniff to her heart's content, but never touch the pie. The adult partridges did quite as much as I towards teaching her to keep her place.

As to the young rabbits, that was not so simple. Their parents have no regard for them after they are three or four weeks old. They throw them out to make room for another family, and from then on they have to fend for themselves. Many of them remain homeless through several months until they secure burrows of their own, and in such a field as the one where Judy and I spent our spare time they provide a recurring temptation to an enthusiastic young dog. My theory was that temptation had to be known at first hand before she could learn to resist it.

Very soon Judy knew the joy of pouncing upon a bunny that had not been quick enough in the take-off, and having the feel of it wriggling and squeaking in her jaws. It was a time for the children's early teaching in the kitchen to be put to the test.

'Fetch it here—to hand!' I said, as all of us had said so often when she brought her dish.

She was very eager to caper and play with it. But Sally and Margaret, to give them credit, had never allowed her to do that with slipper or ball. I had taken them along on many a shooting expedition, and they understood how a retriever was expected to behave. So—a stern word, and Judy let me have the live rabbit. I made her sit, while I placed her catch down on the grass in front of her. Moist and ruffled it panted there for a moment, and then discovered that it was still all whole and complete. It bolted for the nearby marsh. I refrained from grasping Judy's collar.

'Sit there!' I said, very sternly. And she sat.

To drive the lesson home I took the gun out occasionally on those early spring excursions, and shot one or two of the youngsters. Judy was never allowed to touch them, even after they were dead. I kept her at heel while I walked and picked them up, let her have a sniff, and then slipped them into my poacher's pocket.

It seemed important not to hold her collar during any of those exercises, just as I thought it was important to vow at the start that however she might exasperate me—and she did, at times, very thoroughly—I should not put a stick to her hide. It is abominable to go shooting with a man who must hold up the line every half-hour while he catches his dog and leathers it, its yelps warning off every bird for the next mile. Always it is the same man and always the same dog, and neither ever seems to learn anything from the performance. My idea was to get the invisible cord spun, and it meant that only voice or whistle should restrain Judy until such time as she had learnt self-restraint.

Whether I was carrying gun or ash-plant, and whether it was merely a ramble or a deliberate training expedition, I kept an eye on Judy and never let her go beyond the twenty yards without a whistle or a shout. And gradually she came to expect it, and if she did not hear it she would pause and look round, and either wait or come trotting back. Never more than twenty yards without a warning. Never.

Naturally, it did not always work. Often she chased rabbits to their holes. Plainly, at first, she thought the whole world was hers to enjoy. Out in that delightful field we held one-sided conversations that might have come straight from the repertoire of the severest of Victorian fathers. But not the stick, although Judy never knew how near she came, many an evening, to feeling the weight of it across her flanks!

She learned. One day she would be exemplary. On the trail of the partridges she would stop and set me laughing aloud as she tried to achieve the impossible —to let her nose go shooting forward while her pads remained obediently within the limit. The next, she would be off after them in spite of me. But the lawless run shortened.

So we worked, spinning the cord, and it was not always Judy who found it hard to keep the rules. There is something irresistibly amusing in the sight of a puppy racing after a fleeing rabbit, her podgy figure sometimes losing balance and rolling for a yard or two. She was often in danger of being forgiven. But we kept at it, and it took effect, and I hoped the effect would hold when we went out on business in knee-high kale, or chin-high rasp drills, or in the jungle of willow-herb in the spinneys around East Camno, so thick before the snow beats it down that one shooter coming upon another fighting his way through it has been heard to remark: 'Dr Livingstone, I presume?'

And however far short both dog and man may have fallen from perfection, one thing is certain. The pair of us enjoyed it.

The training in the field was not all of it. To another neighbour I was indebted for the right to go as I liked to a half-mile stretch of the river Isla.

For a man with a measure of patience, and endowed with fingers that never feel cold even if they freeze to his gun barrels, that part of that river is paradise.

Wild geese fly over it by the hundred; widgeon in thousands. Mallard rocket up from quiet pools where they have paused to slake their everlasting thirst before supper on the stubble fields. Golden eye pass with their curious, singing flight, and teal with their comical little noises. Occasionally, out of all the multitude, the odd bird offers a shot, and whether it is bagged or not the freezing hour of waiting never seems less than worth while.

I hoped that Judy would become a good water dog; a better one, I dared to wish, than her sire had been.

Danny disliked the river. It had been an effort to train him to retrieve from it. He had in the end come to do it quite well, but I always knew that he was doing it as a duty, uneasily.

We started making excursions to the Isla in the late spring. The children went paddling, and later swimming, and invited the pup to join. The first few times, she dipped a doubtful toe and turned back, shaking it, to dry land. My spirits sank. I was resentful that, having inherited so much from her father, she seemed to have fallen heir to his one outstanding weakness.

Myself, I don't much like the chill of a Scottish river either. But one day when it was low, and the sun seemed warm enough, and the daughters were extra pressing, I took off shoes and stockings and rolled up my trousers and crossed with Sally and Margie.

Back on our own bank, Judy yelped disconsolately. We had made up our minds that she would never be hurled into the water by force, which I am sure is the worst possible kind of start—but now we tried another sort of force. We climbed up the flood-bank and hid on the other side of it.

In no time Judy was beside us, giving us a shower bath.

After that she was quite ready to go swimming, and I started tossing in a stick for her to retrieve. Nothing doing! She would paddle out to it; sniff it; come disdainfully back without it.

So I took a different line. Danny, as I have said, had a passion for water-hens. There are plenty on the Isla. I shot one for Judy, dropping it in mid-stream, and sent her after it. Eagerly she struck out to the centre of the river; took one look, and turned away. Several times I sacrificed a water-hen. Never once would she touch it.

She showed a little more interest when we flung a newly killed rabbit into a shallow, gravelly stretch. She went splashing in—but the rabbit's plimsoll line was, so to speak, somewhere around the base of its funnels. Next to nothing of it was visible as it floated away. Judy pawed and tried to sniff at the place where

Mallard rocket up from quiet pools

it had fallen. She got water in her nostrils, and sneezed, and kept on trying. The rabbit was soon round the bend.

It was no trouble teaching Judy to swim. But training her to swim to some purpose seemed impossible, and suddenly the season was upon me and I had no water retriever. I bought twenty yards of picture cord, hoping that if anything was shot it might be got out by the old stick-and-string method. Judy and I set out for our first evening at the river.

We had scarcely settled in the favourite gap in the bank when a busy, inquiring quacking sounded from the darkling sky. I quacked back an answer, and two of a flight of a dozen mallard broke formation and swung towards the water. I took a crack at the nearer bird.

Let me not seem to pretend to be one of those shooting men who have only to pull the trigger and down comes the quarry—every ball a coconut. Still, there are times when the luck holds, and this night the bird crumpled and fell with a satisfying splash about a hundred yards up-stream. I got out my picture-cord and began fixing a stick on it, while my no-good Judy swam in to investigate.

As she came back, I heard her snorting. I looked on the water—no duck. She brought it to hand as tidily as she had brought her first partridge in the raspberries.

Most of the kindlier spirited writers on dog-breaking advise the use of words of praise as well as words of censure. If your hound deserves it, so they say, let him know of your pleasure. Fuss over him. Pat him. Tell him he has been good.

It is a rule over which no man would quarrel, but it is one which I have never been able to practise. Not, surely, that I am too much of an old grouch to give honour where honour is due. That night, especially, I was all for telling Judy that she was the finest ever. But it was then as it always is. At home, she comes pushing at anyone who will thump and scratch at her. Outside, her mind absorbed in the job in hand, she does not give tuppence for either the friendly phrase or the approving slap.

When I made to pat her and tell her of my satisfaction she dodged indifferently away, as if there were nothing whatever unusual or worthy about her retrieving a duck; as if her feat were a mere matter of routine which she had been performing all her life. Sticks? Bah! Water-hens? Kids' stuff! But duck was duck, and evidently she knew it, although this was the first one she had ever seen.

I got a brace that night, and stuck it out until my bones, as usual, began to feel like icicles within me. As Judy sat beside me after her two dips, her teeth started to chatter in a quaintly human way. It was time to go home, and I set

out willingly, composing lyrics in my mind to the glory of my incomparable
little bitch.

Our way took us across the grass field, the scene of most of the lessons. Judy
got on the scent of one of the partridge coveys. She put them up—and went
barking after them over the breadth of the next three fields. Chasing! And
barking! Incomparable hound?

It might have been that for all her air of indifference she was a trifle cock-a-
hoop. It might have been that she merely wanted to get warm, and so chose
to have a romp in the company of a family who were certainly old acquaintances
if not exactly friends. But I tore up my lyrics, and waited for her, and gave her
as hearty a talking-to as if she had let all the ducks in Perthshire go floating down
the Isla and never put jaw to one of them. It is the only way—never a fault
unmentioned; never, once. Dogs can take it.

But when we reached home, it was only of ducks that I spoke in the family
circle. Not so much as a word about partridges.

When each of those mallard had been brought down again and retrieved
again half a dozen times, I mentioned in a contemplative way that Christmas
would soon be upon us—and that Danny might look the happier for some
company on my study wall.

I knew I had a dog again. A gun-dog.

There is a classic treatise on the art of horsemanship in the circus, *Principes
de Dressage et d'Equitation*, written by James Fillis, who in his day was perhaps
the greatest of all riders in the ring. Fillis wrote:

> 'The highest perfection of the art of equitation, and the ideal for which
> every rider must strive, is a constant and complete mastery over every action
> of his horse. . . . When that is achieved, we see two living creatures welded
> into perfect harmony, and the rider becomes so much a part of his steed that
> he can sense all the impressions it receives. . . . The latter takes their mutual
> understanding for granted, adapts itself to his will, and so attains complete
> agreement with his intentions.
>
> 'From that moment onward, the horse's actions are purely reflex, for
> between the two of them there is only one brain—the rider's.'

The man who is training his own gun-dog should ask for quite as much,
and he can attain it. He will be working with a beast which has a far stronger
instinct to serve him than any horse ever had for any human.

A man's shooting dog should be like another part of himself, and not a personality on its own account. Its hunting should be an act in a piece of mutual activity in which, always, the master's is the leading role. Fully controlled, it will still be happier than a man can ever be, and therefore there is no need to give it any licence for the sake of its own enjoyment. It should be subservient, but never abject; obedient without being cowed; brisk, busy, and insatiably curious in game country, but all its bustle and enquiry confined well within the range of a shotgun. Let it take what delight it gets—and it gets great delight—from its gift of scent. Its nose is its owner's nose.

If any man, without professional help, brings a young dog within striking distance of that ideal, he will have done something as richly rewarding as a free permit to shoot over any thousand acres in the country.

Dogs have minds and ways of their own, in spite of you. But the range of a dog's mind is not so large that it cannot, while on duty, be fully contained within the head of the man who owns it.

'. . . between the two of them there is only one brain . . .'

So, to my fellow shooters, I warmly recommend an effort which will pay rare dividends in a number of ways.

WOODCOCK

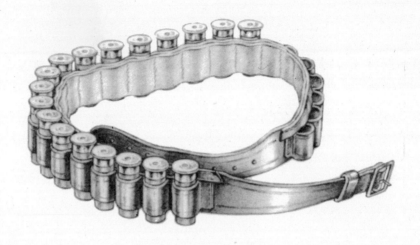

CHAPTER FIVE

HAPPY HUNTING-GROUND

I ONCE shot a robin.

It is true that it was done by mistake. The little fellow happened to get mixed up with a bunch of sparrows which were devouring my hens' corn. I had a crack at them with no. 8 shot from the study window, and when I went to clear away the fifteen corpses—there among them was poor Cock Robin.

I felt like a murderer. Almost any man would. But why? Why so sad for a robin and not for a partridge, which, to anyone who has studied both species closely, is a far more gently mannered and lovable bird?

A man gets hardened. He forgets that the whirring target is a living thing; that the winged bird legging it for cover is a mortal creature like himself whose wounds bleed and sting.

How much longer will it last, this pastime of killing for sport? Four genera-tions? A century, or less? To me it seems certain that it will die out quite soon. The human race is showing signs of becoming civilized, in intention if not yet in practice. Before many years the checking of vermin will be regarded not as a pleasure but as a routine necessity, and the few game birds remaining alive will be left at peace to decorate the landscape.

The whole thing is indefensible. We shooters have the minds and morals of cave-men. But I for one am incorrigible. I think it is wrong, but I still want to go on doing it, and I put this curious confession here on record lest in my old age, when I am too decrepit to enjoy the thrill of it, I am accused of becoming a reformed sinner only when I am incapable of sin. It will die—but it will die hard. Golf is nothing to it. Motoring, tramping, all the other open-air activities —nothing.

It is in the full and unblushing awareness of being more than something of a hypocrite that I plead there is more to game-shooting than the killing of birds and beasts, which can be done twice as easily by the use of traps and snares. There is more also than the stocking of one's larder, which can be accomplished at a quarter of the cost by rearing rabbits and poultry in one's own back yard —or by turning vegetarian and living on cabbages.

One of the best things it offers is the freedom to walk not around but through farmland; not along the edges of the cultivated fields but right amongst the stooks and drills and the sweet, murmurous clover. Lucky the sportsman to whom some part of the earth becomes familiar through the years; who is privileged to watch, as nearly as may be from the inside, the high art of good husbandry and all the multitude of skills that go to make up first-class farming.

Lying on the eastern edge of Perthshire, against the boundary of the County of Angus, is the farm of East Camno. It is part of the estate of Belmont, formerly the home of Sir Henry Campbell-Bannerman and now the property of the Corporation of Dundee. The tenant of East Camno is Alexander Turnbull, who also rents the shooting. There, as guests, Danny and I had our best days. There, when I felt she was fit for it, I planned to let Judy have her first outing in select company.

This man, Alick Turnbull, is of a type which should be better known to my brother-townsman. He is a good farmer.

You, in London, you in Manchester, Glasgow, Birmingham, or wherever it is—at some time or other you have eaten his potatoes, or supped his porridge, or relished his beef or mutton, or sweetened your tea with sugar from his beet.

'Good,' you have said, 'if there were more of it.'

There might have been less.

East Camno is a mixed farm, carrying a large head of livestock as well as arable crops. Each year, if there has been reasonable weather, I have noticed the grass looking a shade greener than the last; the wheat a little taller; the roots rather more difficult to walk through because of the extra luxuriance of their growth. The earth is producing all the time, and yet all the time growing more productive.

So too with the animals—improving, improving. The East Camno flock of

Suffolk Down sheep was established before I first walked across its pastures. They were good sheep then, and they are better sheep now. The buyers at the Kelso ram sales have said so with guineas. I saw the start of the herd of pedigree Aberdeen-Angus cattle, and season by season I have watched it grow, and prodded at the fat calves, and given a passing slap to the shapely cows, and grown accustomed to meeting a thousand pounds' worth of young bull, all inside the one skin. I was acquainted with Belmont Castle, first stallion of the Clydesdale stud, from the day of his birth.

Many astute farmers I know hold that the rearing of pedigree stock is not worth the trouble. They may be right, but it is certainly not true of East Camno, where I am sure it pays handsomely. But whether or not it paid in cash, it gives another sort of return. There is the love of it.

There might, also, be a comforting sense of the importance of it; and it is very important, in a very practical way, to have a hand in making that steak or chop on the townsman's table a little juicier, a little more attractive to his palate, and ready for the pot a week or two sooner.

In the dining-room at East Camno, looking at the glittering array of silver cups and medals and trophies on the sideboard, and knowing the beasts which won them and the man who bred the beasts, I found myself remarking one day:

'I'd still like to be asked to come shooting here, even if I had to carry nothing but blank cartridges.'

But cynics may still detect, in this preoccupation with the other pleasures, the signs of a guilty conscience.

So, on a fine Saturday, to East Camno with young Judy, in the company of other guns and other dogs and all the excitement of a big occasion. The most I prayed for was that she would behave so quietly and modestly that her presence would scarcely be noticed.

We started off across a stubble field and a grass field, driving the birds into the roots. Several coveys rose. The youngster was a little above herself, and looked as if for two pins she would go after them. She would bounce ahead a few paces—and then, within the twenty yards, pause and look back. But not always without an urgent word from her anxious master.

In the grass, a hare rose from right under her nose. Oh, hopeful plans! Oh, imagined unity of mind! At least she did not give tongue as she set off in chase of it. Thank heaven, my first shot rolled it over. The pellets must have whizzed within three millimetres of Judy's ears, and if any other man had fired so close to my dog I should have told him he was no gentleman and refused to go on walking next in the line to him. I had a private word with Judy as she slopped over the job of picking up the kicking hare, keeping it quiet in the hope that the other men would not notice. Of course, they saw it all.

We moved on towards the sugar-beet; as lush a crop as ever I saw, even at East Camno. By now it was full of game; the very place for a novice dog to go crazy with the delight of a hundred crossing scents, and to engulf all memory of discipline.

At the fence, most politely, Judy sat while the guns climbed through. There was a stretch of bare ground where fifty-odd drills of potatoes had been lifted, and then the beet. Nosing about the field-edge as we reloaded, Judy put up a pheasant. It was the typical bird for a moment like that—straight away, easy, but no one quite expecting it.

The gun on my right snapped in a single cartridge and brought it down, but only winged. It picked itself up and set off in a hurry. Judy, seeing it fall and then take to its legs, leapt in the air and almost forgot to bring her ears back.

'Sit down!' I said. 'Sit down!'

No pup of mine was going to be sent on that retrieve into that paradise of smells, to drive out every bit of game we had trudged to collect and to be cursed by the entire gathering.

Judy sat at once, tongue jerking out and in, and cocking up a bright eye at me as if to say: 'All right! All right! Keep your head! I know!'

We shot out the beet field, three dogs working. We saw no sign of the winged cock.

'Might be worth while going back to have a look for it,' said my neighbour who had brought it down.

'Pretty well impossible . . .'

He was not a dog owner. I told myself that he did not appreciate the difficulty of what he was suggesting. But we went, Judy and I. She found the line at once on the bare land, and followed it into the beet. Here, there, and everywhere her head kept bobbing up as she galloped about. It was true that the field had been shot, so she could do no damage, but to give her such licence appalled me after having kept her so carefully under control.

'I must call her out,' I said to my neighbour.

'She might be on the scent of the bird.'

'Not her! She's hunting rabbits.'

So I whistled—and got no response. She might have been too far away to hear, but I did not think so. In any event, she did not come obediently back. I shouted.

Right at the other end of the field she turned, and at each occasional glimpse I got of her among the tall green tops she was nearer. We were keeping everyone waiting. We were making ourselves conspicuous. I was very sorry I had put her in.

Judy emerged from the beet, and paused to look for me.

'She's got it!' my neighbour said.

She was carrying the pheasant, which was still fully alive and pecking at her face. Without any fumbling she brought it to hand.

'That was a good retrieve,' my neighbour said.

'The first pheasant she has ever carried,' I remarked.

She has carried many a one since, and unaccountably lost some others, and at least once I have seen her leap clean over a dead bird lying in a dry ditch while another man's golden labrador wiped her eye by finding it. I hope she carries many more. But so far as I am concerned she will go on bringing that one, that day at East Camno, for as long as I have a mind that can remember.

If it was Sir Henry Campbell-Bannerman who planted those delightful strips of woodland along the boundaries of East Camno, then blessed be his memory. In the company of Alick Turnbull and his other guests I have spent some of my happiest hours in them.

In the season which has just passed—oh, woe and lamentation!—every tree, every branch, every last twig has been cut down, and the ground cleared as bare as a desert. The immense cauldrons of the charcoal-burners are dotted about the denuded land, and the cover is gone. A mouse could not hide there now. But the Corporation of Dundee is a forward-thinking body, and no part of it more so than the department which manages its lands and estates. They do not, like so many others, fell timber and leave a wilderness. No doubt they will replant, and there will be house-room for a pheasant again.

At the north-eastern boundary of the farm is a plantation of tall fir, a roosting-place for flocks of pigeons. Always, a couple of guns go through this wood, whacking with sticks at the tree-trunks. There is a flapping of wings, and a veritable fusillade of shooting from the flanks—and quite often, for all the din and excitement, not a single pigeon is felled. They are adepts at making that quick, dodging turn just at the instant the trigger is pulled. But I remember one,

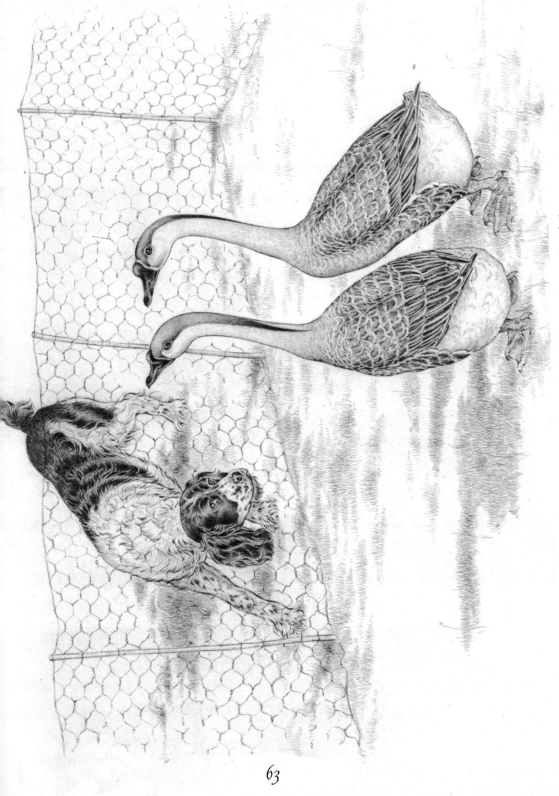

The brace of prisoners stood aloof, forlorn and very dignified

63

and a very high one too, which came down as clean as a whistle to the gun of my friend the doctor.

'Good shot! Oh, good shot!' I said.

'I can hardly believe it myself,' he laughed.

'You're improving!'

'Well . . . I don't know. There was something queer about that bird. Something odd.'

'You needn't be so modest! It was a good shot.'

'But it flew dead-straight. It didn't swerve.'

Judy brought it, and the doctor, who has now given up the joys of a country practice to be an eye specialist in an English city, examined it.

'There—I suspected it,' he said. 'Corneal opacity in the right eye.'

'Corneal . . . what?'

'It has a blind side; the side that was towards me. It didn't see me.'

He took the pigeon home for a post-mortem.

At the farther end of this same plantation there is a curling pond encircled by tall firs, from which, time and again, we saw twenty to thirty mallard take wing as the shooting at the pigeons began.

One day when we were a party of eight we decided to reverse the usual route and try for some of those ducks. We held a conference and laid our plans. This gun was to make a circuit and approach from that side. That one was to creep to a certain point and lie low until the signal was given. Every man was charged with the duty of keeping his dog in control and making his way to his allotted spot at the edge of the pond silently and invisibly. One gun undertook to whistle when everyone was in position. Then we should all spring up, and whichever way the ducks chose to make their exit they would meet gunfire.

Controlling Judy was easy enough. A sporting dog knows just as well as a sporting man the special thrill of a stalk. I have shot thousands of things, but my heart still goes whacking with excitement if I am creeping up behind hedge or wall to get within range of an ordinary, humble rabbit.

My very attitude, bent and picking my footsteps carefully, was enough to tell the yearling springer what was happening. Belly to the ground, and four pads avoiding the crackling undergrowth far more capably than could my two feet, she slid stealthily along at my heel. For once, in the tension, her tail had stopped wagging.

We reached our place. The whistle sounded. With the other seven men

I bobbed up—and shouted with laughter for the sight of a single tiny teal drake in sole possession of the pond. Not a man so much as raised a barrel at it as it fled from the eight assassins.

At East Camno, more than anywhere, Judy learned to be a good enough dog to get by in a company which does not expect perfection, and I, who had come to be on terms of very close understanding with her sire, began to get to know her and her special ways.

It pays a man to keep his eye on his dog most of the time. Its action can convey much information, and there is an endless fascination in trying to interpret its movements. The instant it gets on a scent, one should be aware of it; able too, after a time, to tell what it has scented. It reacts in different ways to different kinds of game.

If it be a partridge covey trying to sneak away in the long stubble, then the trail will be at least a yard wide, and the dog will swing from side to side as he follows it, probably lifting his head now and again to see whether the birds have risen.

If a rabbit is couched somewhere in the grass, the scent seems to spread over an area, and the dog will work his way inwards to it, often lingering behind a too-hurried line.

A hare that has made discretion the better part of valour and, ears flat, has slipped out at one side of the field as the guns entered at the other, leaves a spoor so maddeningly enticing that it will draw any spaniel to the limit of its permitted range in a dead-straight line—and often beyond the limit. A rabbit's escape-route does not make half so urgent an appeal.

Many a time, working Judy along the banks of the burn that runs the full length of East Camno, I have been able to say with certainty to my fellow-guns:

'There's a cock pheasant ahead.'

And at the first break in the cover, up has whirred His Majesty.

The dog's action tells it; not only the line she follows, winding through the long grasses, but also in some subtle way the outward signs of her inner response —the tilt of her nose, the speed of her tail, her whole attitude. It is difficult to define what exactly it is, but there is certainly a visible difference when it is a pheasant as apart from anything else, and even—I am sure of it—a cock as apart from a hen. It is not unlikely that the sexes have their different scents, and Judy must know by this time that while I am ever ready to hunt a square mile of the toughest thicket for the sake of a shot at the gaudy-feathered polygamist, as often as not I will let one of his wives fly free after doing no worse than taking a practice aim at her.

Snipe and woodcock are recognizable too before they make an appearance. They do not run. Both birds have a habit of lying very close. The dog draws on them until it has almost snapped at them—and then up they explode in that teasing zigzag flight which is the despair of other shooting men besides myself. A forewarning of what is coming should be useful. The gun should say to himself: 'I will not fire, I will not fire, until it has stopped weaving and straightened out.' But the first barrel is nearly always wasted.

By working a dog constantly, and studying it as it works, a man can come as near as may be to having a sensitive nose of his own; and the pleasure is such that if there are good shots to right and left one often finds oneself merely carrying one's gun and letting the others do the killing.

A lot of shouting and whistling is disturbing to men and game alike. But there can be no harm in carrying on a quiet, running conversation with a dog as it busies itself in the cover. I do, with Judy. It helps to keep contact. I get no answer but the occasional bright-eyed glance. But it is enough to say that she is keeping me in mind, and that though invisibly attached to a slow, lumbering biped who avoids the best and thickest places—it's fun.

And only fun when that same biped is with her. For at home, although she has full freedom, and birds and rabbits move about their affairs quite near to the house, it never occurs to her to go hunting alone.

A countryman gets to know his dog as no townsman can, simply because, living with it in a more dog-like world, there is so much more to know.

Judy is very close to me, and yet there are gaps in our knowledge of one another. For instance, I cannot understand why, when she sees a dead rat rotting by the roadside, or when the air is pungent with the odour of newly spread dung, she must go and roll on it. Nor does she seem to learn why, when she comes bouncing back to the family fireside stinking to high heaven, she is promptly turned out.

In the shooting field we work in near partnership—but I am still puzzled to know why, like many another dog, she finds snipe and woodcock so revolting. She will put them up readily, but when they are shot she obviously hates to carry them, and even now will sometimes drop them yards from my feet when she would never think of abandoning her hold on any other kind of game until it is safely in my grasp.

Why is it that, however hungry she may be, nothing will induce her to eat the remains of these same two birds, which humans think so clean that they are cooked and carried to the table with the gut still inside them?

No man really knows any man, even himself, so he cannot expect a full knowledge of his dog. But he can come wonderfully near it, and there is a satisfaction in it.

Judy, now, is my shadow; Danny, with a number of others, only a memory. The only privilege of her sire's which has not passed to her is that of spending the empty hours of the working day sprawling on the study floor.

It is not that she is less well liked. It is not that her white hairs show so badly when she drops them on the beetroot-red carpet. It is not that a new rule has gone out, holding just one place in the house free from the intrusion of mud-spreading hounds.

Judy would be welcome, except for one thing.

The instant she falls asleep, she snores.

PTARMIGAN

PART TWO

A Goose in My Hair

CHAPTER SIX

COLONEL HONKY

FOR a short time there was no other dog than Judy at Wester Denhead, but she was never by a long way the only pebble on the beach.

Years ago, on a holiday at Dalwhing, Aboyne, we met an ancient gander named Couthie. This dour old warrior of a bird was too decrepit to move more than a few shaky and painful steps, but in its regal eye there was a curious power. It was the undisputed ruler of the farmyard. By a mere glance it could strike awe into any living thing that ventured upon its kingdom. Even the horses and cattle gave it a wide berth.

We knew Couthie for only a fortnight, but real personality does not need as long as that to stamp its image on impressionable minds. I started having trouble from the moment when the family became acquainted with the King of Dalwhing.

'Oh, Daddy, I wish we had a goose . . .'

If all the wishes were always fulfilled, Denhead would be nothing but a menagerie. Someone has to keep a grasp on the brake handle. The winds of time and fatherly resistance have to winnow the wants. But a few remain to be mentioned again and again until at last, inevitably, they are heard in a moment of weakness.

I know exactly how it happened. I made the fatal mistake of starting an argument.

'Just think—what use would a goose be to you?' I asked, and by 'goose' I

71

took it that Sally meant a gander, like old Couthie. That was what she had meant, too. In all malice it was intended to be a question both unfair and unanswerable.

Sally ruminated over it for a long time, and tried in a tentative voice:

'It would lay.'

'Just like Couthie,' I retorted.

'But I said a goose. I've always said a goose,' she insisted.

She had me there, quite unjustly, on a pure technicality.

'Huge, coarse, uneatable eggs,' I said.

'They're not! They're lovely!' Margie chimed in. 'One would be big enough to make an omelette for us all.'

'You don't get more than a dozen in a season.'

'Well, twelve lunches would be something, and . . . and I just want a goose,' said Sally, and edged disconsolately away. I barked at her as she departed:

'Then why don't you go and look for one?'

The hand on the brake had slipped. I had committed myself, however sourly. From that moment I knew, and so did Sally and Margie, that in due time a goose would make its appearance at Wester Denhead.

The children, with a troop of friends, cycled to all the farms they could think of, and always came back disappointed. Most of our neighbours, it seemed, were wise enough to steer clear of geese. The few who had them were unwilling to part with them.

Yet so much energy and persistence seemed to be deserving of some sort of reward, and although I still could not work up one jot of affection for the goose-to-be, I threw out another hint.

'When I wanted a dog, before I had Danny,' I said, 'I advertised.'

Three days later I was faintly startled to read, among the 'Eggs, Poultry and Rabbits' advertisements in our local paper, a notice saying that I wanted a goose. Never was truth more shamelessly distorted.

After twenty-four hours of expectancy and suspense, there came a letter from Mrs Robertson of Ardblae, Stanley. Mrs Robertson had four young geese . . .

'Oh, Daddy,' said Margie, 'can we have two? I want one of my own.'

'They're twenty-five shillings each.'

'O . . . oh!'

'And I'm not going to pay for one, let alone two. Why should I, when I don't happen to be fond of geese?'

'O . . . oh!'

'But,' I added, 'if there's anything in your money-boxes, I still have the pound apiece Mr Hume insisted on giving you when he had one of Gippy's puppies. It's your cash. You can do as you like with it.'

For the sake of the record, I want to flaunt my own meanness and establish the simple facts. It was not I who bought those geese.

With friend Marjorie for company and as expert adviser, we set out in the car to find Ardblae, Stanley, and after much touring among strange byways and much questioning of everyone we saw, we found ourselves at last on a rough track which appeared to lead nowhere. Across two fields, in a green patch behind a row of isolated cottages, someone was clanking the handle of a big old wooden pump. Four long necks were craning towards the spout of water.

'Geese!'

My passengers scrambled out and went plunging through fences and across field and ditch to inquire whether these were Mrs Robertson's geese, and to ask how a sorely tried motorist might get to Ardblae with due dignity and all in one piece. They came bouncing back, beaming, with a curious piece of information:

'There's no road to the place.'

'Of course there's a road! There must be a road!'

'The people themselves should know! There just isn't.'

And there wasn't. At two field-breadths' distance we had reached as near as motors may to the group of cottages which stand with indifferent backs to the far-off, rutted track, and modest faces turned to the lonely loveliness of a moor. As Mary and I, in our turn, made the venturesome journey towards the pump, I knew that I liked Ardblae. No telephone—that is something to a lover of peace and quiet. But not even a road! Paradise!

Mrs Robertson came smiling out to meet us, and we conducted our business around the pump.

'Which are the geese, and which are the ganders?' Sally asked, with a possessive eye upon the staring quartette.

'It's a goose I want,' said Margie.

'Are they . . . er . . . ordinary geese?' I inquired cautiously. Those long, slim, brown-streaked necks seemed a trifle odd to me.

'They're Chinese geese,' said Mrs Robertson. 'And about which ones are ganders—well, to tell you the truth, I can't be sure. We usually think the biggest ones turn out to be ganders, but I couldn't guarantee . . .'

'Bags me the smallest one!' said Sally.

'Me the next smallest!' cried Margie, and we all helped to drive the four into a corner, grabbing at the convenient handles of those long necks. The chosen two were bundled, hissing, into a pair of sacks. The children had a turn of working the pump, and I cupped my hands and took a long draught of sweet, cold well-water.

With much foreboding I drove the family home. They now owned a pair of geese. Chinese geese. They, not I. But all of us, equally, had to live with them.

In our absence, Grandad had been busy. He had circled fifty yards of wire netting around the dog kennel under the holly-tree on the big lawn. The two writhing, noisy sacks were deposited on the grass. Judy, astonished, sniffed at them and looked ready to run.

We emptied the geese into their improvised pen, and while Judy raced barking up and down, and the children kept their wary ecstasy to the safe side of the wire, the brace of prisoners stood aloof, forlorn and very dignified, surveying Wester Denhead with beady-eyed disapproval.

'What'll we call them?' said Margie.

'Seeing they're Chinese geese,' said I, 'you'd better give them Chinese names.'

'But where can we get Chinese names?'

'Off the tea boxes in the grocer's—those squiggly characters are Chinese.'

'Oh . . . Daddy!'

They searched out the copy of the *Kennel Gazette* in which Judy's registration was recorded. There were chow-names in it, and peke-names, many of them more oriental than China itself. We began to realize, with awe and admiration, how much toil, effort, and ingenuity the breeders of chows and pekes must expend over the christening of their stock. We decided, without asking for leave, to help ourselves.

Sally made a lengthy list of everything that sounded even remotely possible, and then scored out until she had reduced it to three:

Ming Foo; Chunky Lu; Chinkey Poo.

Both she and Margie plumped for Chunky Lu. Chunky Lu or nothing. So I obliged by combing through the pages of pedigrees again, and I found plenty to offer.

'How about this one—Chou Yu?' I asked. 'It's probably what they'll do!'

Stony silence, telling me it was no laughing matter.

'Or Wun Lung Sue?' I suggested. 'Or Wonky Tu? Or this one—this is it! The very thing for the Youngs' Christmas dinner! Yung Chu!'

They were not amused. With 'thank you for nothing' looks they wandered off to argue it out between themselves. But I did not need their thanks. I was rewarded in another way. As I made to close the book my eye lit upon a gem that surely ought to shed its ray upon a wider world. I discovered that one aristocratic peke, that month, had been solemnly entered in the register of the Kennel Club as Wee Tin Po.

When I saw the children again, they had come to an agreement. Sally was sticking to Chunky Lu. Margie, who had heard her bird uttering its first sound other than a hiss since its arrival, had allowed it to christen itself Honky, and I bestowed upon it the rank of Colonel.

It turned out to be a very appropriate name.

We realized from the start that there was a difference between the geese and all the other newcomers which had found themselves transported to Wester Den-head. These two did not dash frantically about, trying to escape. Nor did they seem to mope and pine for the delightful isolation of Ardblae. We saw only an aloof dignity; a long-necked, rigid remoteness; an air of old aristocracy doomed to the guillotine and resolved to betray no emotion.

Because they refused to look downcast they looked, in my wife's eyes at least, pathetic. She bore it for twenty-four hours, watching them from the window as they ignored the lush green of lawn grass, the sparkle of fresh water, the temptations of an assortment of foods among which the sparrows were holding holiday. They did not eat. They did not drink. They did not move by so much as a yard from the spot where they had first been turned out.

On the afternoon of the second day Mary picked up her knitting and a chair. 'I'm going out,' she said, 'to keep them company.'

Close by the water, within the wire-netting fence, she established herself, chatting encouragingly as she knitted. Chunky Lu and Colonel Honky did not need a long campaign of wooing. At once, and wholeheartedly, they accepted Mary's gesture of friendship. They came alive. As if they had only just noticed it, they began gobbling the food that was strewn about their feet. They ducked and splashed in the water, flicking it over their bodies with their mobile necks. And they talked back—low, complacent sounds of comfort and comradeship. When Mary left them at last they raised a protest so loud and shrill that it was heard at Flatfield Farm, almost a mile away.

Judy, of course, had been watching. Nothing can ever happen at Wester Denhead but a dog must have a share in it. As Mary climbed out, Judy sprang in.

She is a sunny-natured creature at all times. Her tail was wagging merrily.

Her barking was pure laughter. There was nothing in her innocent heart but welcome as she edged forward to offer the disarming salute of touched noses.

The geese did not hiss at her. They did not retreat. They merely stood aloof until Judy was near enough. Then, with a quick thrust, Honky struck, and the friendly snout was in the grip of the wicked, saw-edged beak.

Often, since then, Judy has offered to make their quarrel up—although never again by the touch of noses, which is said to be the Chinese way of kissing. She is on the best of terms with everything else at Wester Denhead, but not with Honky. And that, most certainly, is not Judy's fault.

I had been told again and again as I exhausted my arguments against getting a goose that they were no trouble to keep and feed.

'They live on nothing but grass,' Sally had said.

As it turned out, no matter how continuously I kept half an eye on the big lawn from the study window, not once did I see one of the pair nibble so much as a single blade. Corn they would have, or go hungry with a look of martyrdom that was nothing short of blackmail. No other diet passed their beaks until the day when Grandad set about giving Colonel Honky and Chunky Lu a swimming pool.

He rooted out an old tin bath and, scraping the rust from the bottom, discovered that it was peppered with countless holes. It seemed to be beyond all hope of repair. But Sally remembered that they had been damp-proofing the floors of the schoolhouse, and that over the wall from friend Eleanor's garden the workmen had flung an unwanted lump of pitch. It was fetched and set simmering and frothing filthily in a can hung over a hastily lit bonfire. Mine was the duty of wrapping a sack around the boiling can, and pouring the melted pitch thickly over the bottom of the bath.

Honky and Chunky watched, heads tilted, as bucket after bucket of water was splashed in. They could hardly bear to wait. As soon as it was full they waddled forward, and although nothing then nor since would induce them willingly to take a swim, they reached in with their long necks and made a hearty meal of all the pitch they could chip off.

The geese spent their nights in the dog kennel, which has housed some queer tenants but never yet a dog. It was fairly simple to herd them into it of an evening, but getting them out again in the morning was a problem.

For some reason they did not seem to like bringing their heads down to bob

The warm security of what her Scottish grandmother would have called Sally's 'oxter'

77

through the low doorway. They would stay there all day unless I seized one and hauled it out. The other would step forth instantly with a bland look. Then the two, necks outstretched, would move around me, letting out long sounds for all the world like a pair of double bass violinists tuning up. It was a pleasant enough noise, but whatever it meant it was no hymn of thanksgiving. If I stood listening for a moment the pair would set upon my trouser-legs, trying to tear them to shreds.

We had had them for six weeks when Chunky Lu took ill. One morning she (or was it he?) tottered and toppled over and lay helpless on her back, with her feet pedalling the air.

She was carried indoors, established in the clothes basket by the kitchen fire, and surrounded by every possible token of affection. Sally appointed herself chief nurse. Honky made every hour a visiting hour, and dwelt by the back door, letting out piercing calls of comradeship. Every now and then Judy took the chance of administering a consoling lick on the withdrawing head, which Chunky finally thrust into the warm security of what her Scottish grandmother would have called Sally's 'oxter'.

We consulted anyone and everyone who might know about the ailments of geese, and wherever we inquired we got exactly the same advice as our old friend Sandy Ritchie offered.

'Thraw its neck,' said Sandy.

But we gave Chunky her chance, and after ten days, her head resting again in that cosy sanctuary, she died in the presence of the entire family. I buried her at the spot in the garden where I had planned to grow the next season's marrows. In due time they turned out to be whoppers.

So began Honky's solitary rule. So did Wester Denhead fall under the sway of a dark, malevolent dictatorship. Never was nature more narrow and spiteful, more mean and surly, more watchful for the chance of giving a malicious stab in the back.

With one exception, there is not another creature which may live within the tyrant's sight. Judy dare not enter the house while Honky keeps guard at the door. No visitor arrives but is greeted with raucous abuse and that neck-stretched, waddle-footed 'Charge!' which reminds us so acutely of the character in *Arsenic and Old Lace*.

Never have we seen the first sign of one of those outsize eggs, each big enough to make a family omelet. Long ago we realized that Colonel Honky was a gander.

He screams for food, and attacks the lackey who carries it to him. Remorse-lessly he goes for the children, and sends them squealing indoors. We can scarcely look the postman in the face, nor the milkman, nor the girl who drives the laundry van, nor any of the people whose duty brings them about our home. Honky has declared war on them all. Some of our most cherished personal friends ring us up in advance of a visit and ask:

'Will you shut Honky up in the garden?'

Only towards Mary does he show that even the wickedest of natures can hold one spark of goodness. Can it be possible that he still remembers the day when she took her knitting out to keep him and Chunky Lu company?

For her he tunes his double bass on a wholly friendly note whenever she pauses to talk to him. He will follow her anywhere and everywhere, all but tumbling over her heels. Many a time passers-by on the Aberdeen–Perth road or down on the river bank must have been surprised to see the ungainly figure panting after her as she went walking.

He likes Mary without qualification, and all the rest of his affection, such as it is, is reserved for the one-gallon galvanized watering-can which usually sits under the back porch. Each day he comes round to talk fondly to it for half an hour; and then, when it fails to answer, he sets upon it and does his best to destroy it.

Of course, like all the other pets, he has found his way into the kitchen. But Honky is not satisfied, as are bantams and rabbits, hedgehogs and white mice and the rest, to forage round for pickings and then to enjoy a quiet bask at the warmth of the range. Honky must move with every movement of the mistress of the house as if he were tied to her—from sink to stove, from stove to dresser, through every passage and room if he were allowed, close to her feet.

That he is not allowed is purely his own fault. So far, we have not discovered the secret of house-training a goose.

Why, then, do we keep this monster?

'He's a better watch-dog than Judy,' Sally pleads, and indeed he is. Visitors may not approach Denhead without Honky telling the world of their coming.

'He's good fun at the river,' says Margie, and that I cannot deny. He has only to be lifted over the fence of our neighbour's grass field, and he will jog contentedly by Mary's side all the way to the water. There he drops his vices and, paddling and swimming with Judy and the children, he makes a better plaything than any inflated rubber toy.

They dive under him and catch him. They swim with one arm around him. They splash him, race him and chase him, and he seems to enjoy it all. They used to persuade me at times to put him in a box on the back of the car and carry him off—honking every time the horn sounded—to some of the more distant swimming places on the Tay or up Glenshee.

'You can't deny you're fond of him yourself!' Sally accuses, regarding me with a too-knowing eye. 'Remember that day with the cattle?'

I remember. We were at the river. The cattle which graze the bank came snooping along as cattle will, full of curiosity. Usually it is the dog that draws their notice, but for once they ignored Judy. She was quite a commonplace figure on the landscape. The whole company, to a beast, wanted to investigate this new, feathered oddity.

They circled around Colonel Honky, who had never before given us a hint that he could fear man, beast or demon. On a sudden decision, from all sides they charged. I sprang forward in a consternation which my elder daughter did not fail to notice. For a second or two it seemed certain that the peppery Colonel had met his doom.

We had forgotten that he is, after all, a bird. With a thrashing of his wings and a terrified cry he just managed to lumber over the backs of the attacking herd and land clattering in the midst of our picnic spread.

'He's rather quaint, you know,' says Mary, as she tries to improvise barrers to keep him out of the house.

I am silent. I say nothing whatever. Never a word did I say even when Mary, looking over the answers to a magazine quiz, announced with more than a trace of awe that barring accidents a goose may live for fifty years.

Fifty years! And a so-called life sentence is only fifteen!

CHAPTER SEVEN

WINDOW GAZING

THIS disturbing element, this tantalizing and enticing fresh air, can be shut out by snibbing the window firmly down. But a man who was really serious about eliminating all the distractions that lift his nose from the grindstone would go one better. He would fit panes of frosted glass.

A remarkable number of interesting things can happen within view of a farm-house window. The aggressive face of a gander is not the only one that comes peering in at mine.

Not far from us is a big estate where pheasants by the score stroll around, as casual and as numerous as poultry. Often, very often, one of them goes a-roving, and there he is with the sunlight glinting on his showy feathers as he pecks among our beech-nuts or stops to crow a challenge from the edge of our little field.

For some, the mere sight of so fine a bird would be enough. It would be pleasure and to spare just to look at his vivid plumage and to watch him strutting with his grand, lordly air. But not so when he comes to Wester Denhead.

If it is the season, he has to be stalked. Usually he manages to make his escape, leaving nothing behind but his scent to titillate Judy's nose. But not always! Many a one has offered an awkward, swinging shot through trees or hedge, and finished his excursion in our larder, a hook through his beak. In the country you take what comes your way.

Pigeons, wild duck, woodcock, partridges, rabbits and hares in plenty, and one memorable day a capercailzie—all these have wandered within twenty yards of my study window. Not always is the gun seized, but at the very least they demand to be looked at.

Other gentry pay calls too—kestrels and sparrow-hawks that set the bantams churring angrily and scampering for the field hedge, although they are never attacked; a brown squirrel skipping among the winter branches; a daytime owl with all the birds of the district mobbing him; a mole blundering blindly about searching for a hole to take him back to the familiar darkness of the underground; and, of course, the countless small birds. It is not good business, sitting staring at them, but it sometimes seems like good living.

I remember with what delight I once saw a small brown weasel having a merry game on the lawn. It was a breezy day in April; the kind of day when the feel of the pregnant air penetrated even through glass and cigarette smoke. Colonel Honky was not on sentry duty. Leaves were dancing about, and the weasel was capering after them.

They are cheeky enough, the weasel tribe, not to care even if they know they are being observed. They love to play to an audience. But this one was not self-conscious. He was the very embodiment of all the joy of spring as he captured the flying leaves, and let them go, and bounced after them again. He went prancing up the see-saw plank, and gave a skip and a turn and down again, a picture of innocent happiness.

Had he been a rat, however jolly-spirited, I should have taken the gun and eased the window up, and blown his whiskers off. But I should no more have thought of shooting the merry weasel than if he had been a blue-tit or a puppy.

I wish I had been less soft-hearted!

That evening when I went to feed old Mopsy, he was lying stiff in his hutch with two small punctures at the back of his neck.

The children were without a rabbit. They had a dozen other pets, but still: 'The place doesn't seem right without a rabbit.'

When Sally had her next birthday she found, among the parcels, a ball of string. She looked at it curiously, with its coloured label, as she unwrapped this and that. Finally, when everything else had been discovered, she picked it up and read the label.

'With love from Daddy. X X X.'

'Well,' she said gallantly, 'it's a very useful thing. I'm always wanting a bit of string. A whole ball, all to myself!'

Very gallantly!

She noticed that it was partly undone, trailing on the floor. She began winding it up, and discovered that the loose end was somewhere beyond the dining-room door; somewhere under the hall rug; somewhere down the passage towards the back door; somewhere . . .

It led her, winding with increasing suspicion and excitement, to the coal-shed and the pump-house and right around the garden, and finished up in the summerhouse where Flopsy, with a litter of seven, was waiting to fill the gap which the weasel had left.

A very poor idea, and one which I had cause to regret.

No living thing is prettier or daintier than a baby rabbit at about three weeks old. But how they grow! And how they eat! Soon, in my twice-a-day round of the menagerie, I found the feeding of eight fat, voracious rabbits nothing but a tyranny.

'You'll have to give some of them away!'

But other parents are wiser than I. Although they were offered 'free to good home', only a couple were accepted. I still had half a dozen to provide for. It was five too many.

'Tame rabbits,' I remarked meaningly, 'are bigger and plumper than wild ones—and tastier.'

At the next feeding-time, Flopsy was alone in the hutch. Judy gave chase to something among the trees, and caught and brought me a nicely marked Dutch rabbit.

'They'll be pretty,' I was told, 'hopping about the place. And they'll easily feed themselves.'

Truly, they were pretty. It was a pleasure to see them about. But it was the story of the ten little nigger boys all over again. Four of them came to bad ends, one by one. The last survivor dodged around for a long time. When it managed to elude Honky's malevolent eye, its favourite shelter was under the end of the see-saw plank. It never learned to scrape a hole for itself, nor even to use any of the ready-made holes in the wood.

But it learned something else which, mercifully, has so far defeated the intelligence of the wild rabbits. It got the knack of climbing the fence into the garden.

In winter I did not begrudge it the odd nibble at brussels sprout or swede, but with the spring, and good fresh grass in plenty everywhere, I was not disposed to be so lenient. Then, a whole row of young sprouts was only a single meal.

'It has to go . . .'

It defied all my efforts to catch it. I set Judy after it, and right heartily she did her best, but it knew exactly where to go to elude her.

'I'll have to shoot it . . .'

But before the gun had been loaded, there it was hopping around the kitchen.

'How on earth did you manage to get hold of it?'

'Goodness, it's quite tame!'

Fussing over it, the daughters discovered that it was infested with fleas. So they fell upon the cake of sheep-dip which is kept for the carrots (and which never prevents their being wiped out by the fly) and mixed up a strong-smelling brew and gave it a bath. It was presented with the name of Mopsy.

Twenty-four hours after it had been caught and de-loused and housed, it was discovered fussing over a nest of fluff in a corner of the new hutch. A litter of nine, varying in looks from the pure wild to the pure Dutch.

For six weeks they were nourished on the fat of the land, and cleaned and tended. Then, on a day when the children were lunching at school, I had each of them out of his fur coat in a twinkling.

Let the Americans go into ecstasies over their chicken Maryland—there is no more toothsome food in this world than fried baby rabbit. Mary and I managed the nine between us. A dish fit for a king!

We made no bones about it when Sally and Margie came home.

'We ate them!' I said.

They are country children, and have to be hardened to the realities of country life.

They frowned a bit, and listened poutingly as I expanded upon the flavour, the savour, the succulence. Then, in unison, they attacked me for my heartlessness.

'You might have kept some for us . . .'

Not always does the wandering pheasant find itself stalked and popped at. I have a pious rule that I never shoot hen-birds around home, and, of course, we have visits when the season is past.

For some weeks we were awakened each morning by a cock pheasant crowing on the lawn, right under the bedroom window. It is a harsh and grating sound, lacking any music, but it has its charm for people like us. This gentleman seemed to know quite well that he was protected by the law and the date. When he saw me peering out at him he did not beat a hasty retreat, but merely bobbed, tail up, to the other side of the hedge, and crowed again.

Just at that time we were preparing to go to Aviemore on a long working holiday, of which more anon. Grandad and his faithful Mrs Boucher came to take charge of the place and the livestock, and both were pleased to hear of the visiting cock. But its significance did not strike them, nor us, until we were away. It only dawned when we had a letter from Grandad telling us how everything was faring. One of his sentences read:

'We are certain that that little demon of a Penny is off sitting on a nest somewhere, but although we have hunted high and low, we can't find it.'

We sympathized. Penny the bantam was always a genius at hiding her nests. Usually they are found the following year—a mass of yellowed eggs. But another item in the same letter suddenly linked itself with that one:

'It is several days now since the cock pheasant has come crowing to wake us. We miss the old fellow.'

Could it be? We made hasty inquiries, and discovered at Aviemore a countryman who was prepared to swear that pheasants can mate with domestic poultry and produce fertile eggs. He said that it had happened within his own experience, and that he had been successful in rearing some of the crosses. We hurried back to our hotel to send off instructions to Grandad and Mrs Boucher. If the impossible happened and they did discover Penny's hide-out, on no account was she to be disturbed.

Over that evening's meal we speculated happily on our newest pets-to-be. What would they look like? How would they behave? Would they be wild or tame?

And what should we call them? Pheasbants? Bantpheases?

'Phantoms?' suggested Sally.

'The very word! Phantoms . . . poultrygeists . . .'

In the morning, while our letter was being carried south, another one arrived from Grandad—from the one-time sleuth; the expert finder-out of secret affairs; the tracker of doers of clandestine deeds.

'Penny certainly had us baffled. Three mornings when she came to breakfast we tried to follow her, and she managed to slip away through the hedge and out of sight. But today we played a trick on her. We caught her and shut her up for a couple of hours. When we let her out she was in such a hurry to get back to her nest that there was none of the usual dodging. She took wing and flew straight down to the straw in the old round tower at the steading. She had nine eggs. Mrs Boucher made a delicious omelet . . .

And that was the end of our brood of phantoms. Phantoms indeed!

From my study window, during the first weeks of a certain May, I kept seeing a hen pheasant come running across our two-acre field and disappear through the hedge and over the drive. Plainly, she had a nest hidden somewhere.

A section of the wood was marked off as out-of-bounds to dogs, children, and all others, and the nose kept lifting from its grindstone a hundred times of a morning as I watched for the lady slipping off to breakfast. As soon as she had gone, Mary and I would hurry down and search among the tangle of ground-ivy, daffodil leaves, and grass. The nest was as difficult to find as the worst of Penny's. We did not come upon it until we had hidden ourselves among the bushes and set watch for the hen's return. There were fifteen eggs, cunningly concealed among the ivy.

When the children heard of it, they had an idea.

'Jenny's broody,' they said. Jenny was a third bantam, and a very handsome one, who had been presented to us. 'Take some of the pheasant's eggs and let her sit on them!'

Carelessly I let drop another idea.

'And get some fertile bantam eggs from somewhere, and fill up the pheasant's nest with those?'

They were all for it. There was no peace until we had set off for East Camno, where we had seen a pen of bantams beside one of the cottages. Luckily, their owner was not at home—I half-regret it still, although I have an uneasy feeling that it would have been bad manners to play a trick like that on my neighbouring countrymen, not to mention the unsuspecting hen pheasant.

We did, however, help ourselves to seven of her eggs, and were relieved to find that she had not noticed the robbery. Brooding pheasants are the fussiest of all birds, and will desert their nests for the slenderest of reasons.

Our pretty Jenny accepted the eggs, which were carried to her warmly wrapped in cotton wool and placed for her in a cosy basket on the bottom shelf of the linen cupboard.

We had made a careful note of the day when the pheasant began to sit. Hen-eggs, of course, take three weeks to hatch. When the twenty-seventh day had passed without a cheep, we decided that the experiment had been a failure. We filled a basin with lukewarm water and, remembering an expedition we had once made in search of gulls' eggs, we did our best to test the pheasant's.

The gamekeeper who had rowed us out among the screaming gulls had said, as we recalled it, that if the eggs sank to the bottom of a bucket of water and lay flat, they were fresh. If the broad ends tilted upwards, they contained chicks. If they floated, they were rotten. Our pheasant eggs floated, but each with its broad end upwards.

'There are chicks in them,' said the children.

'They're rotten,' said I, and to prove it I took one of the seven and broke it. Inside, fully developed, was a baby pheasant. Thus we learned that they take a month.

Two days later Jenny hatched the other six. She seemed quite satisfied with her brood. The children were delighted. Myself, I had bleak memories of other impulses which had ended in much the same way . . . not with an ending, but with a beginning. Getting possession of living creatures is fatally easy. Once got, they have to be looked after. I now had the care of six young pheasants on my hands.

'They're very difficult to rear,' everyone told me.

'You'll never do it,' they said.

Somewhere I had read that newly born partridges are unable to survive unless, during their first few days, they can feed on ants' eggs. Ants' eggs, or death—so some writer had given me to understand. Whether or not the same applied to pheasants I was not sure, but I was taking no chances. I wanted those cheepers to live.

We put Mopsy in beside Flopsy and stole her five-windowed bungalow, which we carried into the garden. None of us could remember having seen a single ant there.

'But there are greenfly, and carrotfly, and blackfly, and butterflies and caterpillars,' said Sally. 'Won't they be enough?'

'Ants' eggs—or death.'

'If you have a goldfish,' said Margie, 'you can buy them in packets from the dog-food shop. I wish we had a goldfish . . .'

'Packets! Dried-up things! They want them fresh, and living.'

It might not be so, but there was no sense in taking risks when I knew a spot where the mossy red stones of an ancient dike lay tumbled about the roots of a row of wild cherry trees; a spot where I had often sat with my gun commanding a rabbit warren, waiting to get a supper for the dogs. It would have been a comfortable and delightful place but for the myriads of ants crawling up the legs of my trousers. It is always an advantage to know your countryside.

We set off for the fallen dike, and luckily the two daughters are not fastidious about handling things that crawl and squirm. We grubbed the stones up and tumbled them over, and soon we had as fine a collection of ants' eggs as was ever set before any family of pheasants. We snatched virgin-white grubs from the arms of the flurried nurses who were hastily carrying them to safety. We scooped up fistfuls of earth and roots fairly crawling with ants and their progeny in all stages of development. We carried a large tinful back to Jenny and emptied it on the floor of her bungalow. At once she began scratching delightedly amongst the mess, and calling to the cheepers.

By bad luck, the first three days were bleak, cold, and very blustery. Three times did I bring a supply of ants' eggs, and three times did I find a chick missing. I knew they could not have gone far. I hunted the garden, listening intently for a disconsolate cheeping. But the clamour of the wind killed every other sound. Not a trace was ever found of the three.

'You'll never do it . . .' they had said.

But three remained. Even fifty per cent, we decided, would be a triumph.

The weather mended, and wherever they were in the garden the chicks were able to keep contact with Jenny. We found that from their earliest days they were far more independent than ordinary chickens. They did not bunch close to the bantam, leaving her to do all the work, but went scampering off alone to leap at flies and search the leaves for insects. Watching their wanderings within the confines of the garden, and remembering the three which got lost in the storm, we found it hard to understand how a wild pheasant, with all the countryside free to her, can ever keep her brood together.

We realized very soon that we could hardly have done worse than choose Jenny as foster-mother to the pheasants. She is a charming bantam, very good-looking, beautifully feathered, and with a dainty double comb. She is as tame and friendly as any bird could be. When she is laying, she will lay nowhere but indoors. She loves to get among the dishes when they are piled ready for washing by the kitchen sink, to peck at scraps. If she is lifted away from them she will cackle a protest and go straight back, clambering over the hand that tries to restrain her.

As a dainty and lovable pet, no praise is too high for her. But as a mother, she deserves no less than six months in Holloway on a conviction for gross and heartless neglect.

Ten days old our pheasants were—ten days, and not another hour—when we found the three mites huddled together under a plum tree in the branches of which the callous Jenny had gone to roost for the night. It is true that she abused us in gutter-language when we came handling her family and trying to make things more comfortable for them, but when I got the step-ladder to have her down and put her about her duties, she merely flew into the next tree and cackled her insults from there. If the children could not come upstairs to bed, she seemed to be saying, she was darned if she was coming down.

We could not catch her, and neither did we manage to put the family up beside her. The best we could do was to improvise a shelter of sacks, sticks, and straw—and the little pheasants ran out of that as fast as we could put them in.

'Very difficult . . .' they had said. Very!

But not impossible. For, by some miracle, the three survived. Jenny abandoned them completely within another week and, friendly as we felt towards the infant game birds, we could not spend the whole day herding them and discovering insects for them. We gave them scraps and crumbs and left the rest to themselves. They proved to be far less helpless than we had been led to understand.

They were born on the third of June. On the thirteenth they were noticed taking their first flight, box-hedge-hopping across the garden path. Within a short time the garden wall meant nothing to them. They could go skimming over it at will out into the raspberry fields, and we did nothing to hinder their comings and goings. They were as free as the other eight which their true mother had hatched.

From the beginning, one had been considerably bigger than the other two. We decided that we had a cock and two hens. At eight weeks old we were certain. The big one began to show red around the eye, and soon afterwards his plumage feathers were growing. We were able to study them closely and affectionately, for, although their power of flight enabled them to get farther away, faster, when they were alarmed, they were almost as tame as the bantams.

They would eat out of the children's hands

91

To me as a shooting man, those three birds were a special and peculiar delight. It never seemed less than a miracle to go out into the garden and call, and see pheasants come planing over the wall and land at my feet; flying towards me trustingly, instead of away in panic. They would hop up on to the stone slab by the kitchen window which serves as a bird table, and eat out of the children's hands. For the first time we were seeing pheasants at close quarters— alive. The increasing beauty of the cock, and the modest trimness of the hens, was a daily joy to us.

Dog Judy, although they had been reared under her nose, thought the whole thing very odd indeed. She never mistook them for poultry, nor did she ever get accustomed to picking up their scent in the garden. Always it excited her. Always, eagerly, she told me there were pheasants about. Countless times she went dashing among the cabbages and put them up, waiting for the shot and watching for one of them to fall. Her harrying did not seem to trouble them. They realized that their wings were defence enough against her exuberance, and they always came back.

'What will happen when the shooting season opens?' the children began to ask.

'The hens will be safe enough,' I assured them. 'As for the cock . . . well, if he doesn't wander too far, he'll not come by any harm either. This year, I'll not touch any cock that rises anywhere near the house.'

'Couldn't we catch him and mark him?' they suggested. 'It would be easy to put a ring on his leg.'

'You ought to know that they tuck their legs in when they're flying. I'd never see it.'

'What if you shoot him, then?'

It was an oddly uncomfortable thought, but I was determined that even if it were to cost something to the larder and to the winter's sport, that bird should live.

The harvest was cut and carried. The three learned to fly out of the safe cover of the raspberry drills and to know the delight of their kind in the bounty of the stubble. The first of October arrived, but I did not go foraging as usual for the first pheasant of the season. I was too anxious lest I might bag my own young cock.

And all the time, at the back of my mind, I was well aware that I am not the only man in this district with an eye for the attractions of game birds.

I am not the only man who owns a gun.

The first Sunday of that October dawned bright and clear; the sort of morning, had it not been the Sabbath, to tempt a man from his bed to go for a pre-breakfast tramp with a gun under his arm. I was lying looking out at the early sunlight caressing the old larches on Gask Hill when I heard a shot. Judy in the kitchen had heard it too, and began to bark.

It was a modest, unostentatious shot which might have been mistaken for the backfire of a distant car; might have been, but was not, although it had not gone off with the frank, full-throated crack of a twelve-bore. It was the secretive voice of a four-ten. And it was very close at hand.

I sprang out of bed and ran to the window. After a moment a man passed along the main road. He was walking at a good pace, and yet not in obvious haste. As he went spanking back towards Coupar Angus he looked about him in a way which might have been called furtive. He had a bulge in his coat, just above his left hip. He was carrying a stout walking-stick.

He was carrying it in an odd way; not swinging and swishing it merrily through the sweet morning air, nor thumping it on the roadway at every other step, but wearing it hooked over his arm.

I dressed in a hurry, and went to the garden with a bowl of scraps, and called the pheasants. The two hens came flying over the wall, ready for breakfast. But no cock in the full glory of his adult dress. He never came again.

The following Sunday, the very same performance was repeated—the discreet cough of a four-ten; the figure hurrying without haste; something bulging under the coat; the walking-stick carried over the arm.

And at breakfast-time, only one hen pheasant flying to my feet for crumbs.

We pondered over it during the week. We discussed it with sympathetic friends.

'The only thing to do,' said some, 'is to make a wire cage and keep the last one in that.'

'If you clipped one wing,' others offered, 'she could not get out of the garden.'

But we had no notion whatever for a pheasant in a cage. Nor did we have much for a pinioned bird running around the garden, deprived of the one supreme advantage which the fowls of the air have over men. The essence and the symbol of the pleasure we had had in them was the sight of pheasants flying from complete freedom towards us instead of away from us; flying, at a call, from the wild world, to eat out of the children's hands.

I would have no cages, and no clipped wings.

On the Saturday, anticipating the Sunday morning stroll of the character whose walking-stick concealed the barrel of a four-ten gun, I went out with Judy. From the grassy bank on the edge of the stubble field she put up a hen pheasant. I shot it, and tied a label to its neck, and posted it off to one of the grandfathers.

We shall not rear pheasants again.

PHEASANT

CHAPTER EIGHT

HARDY LADIES

YEARS ago we went into the pros and cons of poultry-keeping, and decided to have none of it. Hens were a tie. They made a place look untidy. Houses and wire cost a ransom. The creatures were always dying of paralysis, coccidosis, and a multiplicity of ailments. So, for Wester Denhead—no fowls. One ill-humoured gander was more than enough in that line.

When Blackie and Penny, the first of the bantams, sneaked into the household under the heading of 'pets', we did not realize what we were starting. However commonplace a thing it may be, there is still something of magic in turning an egg into a live chicken. The daughters found it irresistible.

They set Blackie upon a single egg in the kitchen. She hatched out a cockerel which, when he had grown to a plump eight pounds, we promptly

96

ate. The following year, searching for a shirt in the linen cupboard, I came upon Blackie sitting on three full-size eggs, and close beside her was Penny on another three.

The result of these efforts was one incredibly bad egg which finished by exploding stinkingly on the kitchen floor; three more excellent dinners—and Comfy and Clucky. These last two managed to survive, and I was made to understand that they were no concern of mine. They were not to be regarded as poultry. They, too, were pets.

They had no house. They roosted in the yew trees.

'That's all very well in the summer,' I declared. 'But when the hard weather comes, they're not to be taken indoors to perch on the clothes-pulley with the bantams. Then—they're for the pot.'

Long before the earliest sign of snow, Clucky came stepping into the kitchen and, settling in Judy's chair, laid her first egg. It was an unusually dark brown egg, very luscious-looking, and when it had been hard-boiled and meticulously halved, it was pronounced the best ever.

Comfy was only one day behind. In she walked, singing to herself, the next morning, very red in the comb and with a slightly perturbed manner. She was discovered on top of the electric cooker looking speculatively into a saucepan. She was presented with a box marked 'Best Fillets', lined with a cot-size eiderdown and therein she obliged.

'Oh, Daddy, you couldn't kill two laying hens . . .'

'Wait till the hard weather, and you'll see!'

A few days later I found a surprise on my breakfast plate. There, in an egg-cup, was a gaudily painted Humpty Dumpty, and lying beside him, grinning from ear to ear, his twin brother. Although they were smiling so merrily, their hands were clasped in supplication, and each bore, printed round his collar, the message: 'Please spare my mother!' I knocked their heads off, and ate them. Delicious!

'Daddy, you couldn't . . .'

So there we were—two hens.

In November they moulted, and that was the end of the egg-laying for the season. The hard weather came—frost, snow, icy gales. Each night Comfy and Clucky went to roost in the yews, and many a morning I expected to find them dead of the cold. They proved as hardy as the robins and sparrows which shared their frigid dormitory. They survived, as everything does at Wester Denhead, wanted or unwanted.

7

In May of the following year the children heard of Mr Cunningham. He was a stranger to us, but they had noted down his name and address, and they were determined to be taken visiting him.

'We've never seen a place like that,' they pleaded. 'He has thousands and thousands of chickens hatching in incubators. Couldn't we go, and see?'

Vainly did I plead that men who have thousands of chickens to attend to have no time to waste on idle visitors.

'But we wouldn't expect him to show us round. We only want to look. Do ring him up and ask if he'd mind!'

Mr Cunningham didn't mind. We drove up to his trim, attractive home to be greeted by two useful-looking, dark brown spaniels, and to be taken at once to the hatching-shed which was filled with the little, complacent noises of multitudes of newly born chicks. We saw hundreds of pure-bred ones of various sorts, and hundreds of sex-linked crosses, the pullets distinguishable from the cockerels as soon as they stepped out of the egg. Mr Cunningham answered a battery of questions, and asked one of his own:

'Haven't you any hens at home?'

'We have two—and one of them is broody.'

This was news to me. Suspicion had hardly had time to take shape when:

'Oh, Daddy, I wish we could get some chicks for Clucky!'

At once, Mr Cunningham sprang to my aid. He pointed out that all his day-olds were on order, and showed a pile of hay-lined boxes already packed and waiting to be delivered. As the two faces fell, he added:

'I might manage to scrape up half a dozen pullets, but they'd be a scratch lot, not all of the same breed.'

'It would be nice,' said Sally, 'to have them different.'

When we set off for home, we carried six day-old pullets cheeping in a cardboard box.

'Try the hen with one, at first,' Mr Cunningham advised. 'If she seems willing to take to it, give her the others.'

'And if not?' I turned to the daughters. 'You'll have to learn to cluck, and brood them yourselves!'

'If not,' said Mr Cunningham, 'wait until it's dark, and try again.'

We carried the tweeting box to Clucky's nest, which was on top of a barrel in the tool-shed. Gingerly I grasped one of the chickens and made to pop it under her wing. Not so simple! She fluffed her feathers up in a fury; pecked to draw blood; caught hold of my jacket sleeve with her beak and shook it as viciously as a terrier shakes a rat. The chick vanished under her. Scratched and gory, I went in search of a pair of stout leather gloves.

Clucky did not seem to have any objections to the new family as they were pushed one by one into the shelter of her wings. Her whole idea was to tear me to shreds. She was panting with rage and excitement, her tongue jerking out and in like a breathless dog's.

We drew back and watched. All was well for a time. Then one chicken poked an inquiring head from under the protective wing. Clucky seized it in her beak and dropped it overboard on to the flag-stoned floor. Hastily we took the helpless babes away from her and waited until midnight, when we went through the whole performance again.

In the morning she was chatting affectionately to her brood, and went for us violently when we tried to take a peep at them.

We had been determined not to be poultry-keepers. But now we had two hens, two bantams, half a dozen pullets, and one dark-spirited Chinese gander which never lost a chance of trying to annihilate all the others. But let the truth be confessed—that scratch lot from Mr Cunningham's hatchery very soon convinced us that it would be senseless to live in the country without a few hens pecking around the door.

Colonel Honky had always objected to being put to bed in the dog-kennel. Usually it was necessary to imprison him by force. So we presented it to Clucky and her family, and at once the villainous gander took a great liking to his old home and would go charging at the door, trying to batter his way in.

He was so troublesome that after a month of foster-motherhood and many a valiant fight with him Clucky gave up the struggle and went back to her old draughty perch in the yew trees, twenty feet up. Somehow the chicks managed to scramble from branch to branch until they were beside her, pushing and thrusting in their efforts to get close. It took them the better part of a couple of hours, with many fluttering falls back to earth, before they arranged themselves as neatly and sensibly as any human mind could have planned. Two parked themselves on either side of Clucky under her outspread wings, and two managed somehow to get between her legs. Then peace settled over the hen-roost.

It looked very uncomfortable for the hen. She stuck it for a fortnight, and then she had had enough of this nightly jostling and shoving and jockeying for position. Like Jenny with the pheasants she gave the whole thing up; pecked the chicks when they came near her, and turned them into orphans.

'Poor little mites!' said the children, and set about fixing a perch in the linen cupboard, just under the hot-water tank, with a newspaper carefully spread over the shelf below. But their mother was having none of that!

Nevertheless, they survived. In the fields around us the raspberries ripened. We fed the chickens well, and did our best with two rolls of wire-netting, but they were always breaking out and going to forage on the land of our fruit-farming neighbour. We tried to believe that they were only seeking insects and weed-seeds, but we could not help noticing that some of the spurs of raspberries grew very low.

Uneasily and apologetically I spoke to my neighbour. He looked at me with hardly a hint of a twinkle in his eye.

'I don't think a rasp or two should do them any harm,' he said.

He was kindlier, if no pawkier, than the man who prepared a special meal for the next-door chickens which were raiding his garden. This man drilled a quantity of grains of maize, and to each tied a label with six inches of thread. That evening the poultry owner found every one of his fowls with a message dangling from its beak:

'I've been a naughty bird. Please keep me at home in future in case I get killed.'

We propped up our makeshift fence, and the fruit season passed, and if the pullets did have a few raspberries they came to no harm.

It was one thing having a couple of casuals like Clucky and Comfy lodging in the yews; it seemed quite another matter now that we had a flock of poultry. Whether or not it was going to cost a ransom, they had to have a decent home.

Years of record-breaking egg-laying would not have paid for any henhouse we found for sale.

'I'll make one myself,' I vowed.

But the price of timber added up to a sum almost as fabulous as what was being asked for the finished job, and besides, it was not merely a case of ex-changing some cash for some boards. There were permits to be obtained; forms to be filled in.

I am not one of those who grumble about form-filling. It is a fascinating pastime. Because we have a two-acre paddock we are listed as farmers, and are called upon to make as many and as comprehensive returns as if we cultivated half of Perthshire. The curiosity of the Scottish Department of Agriculture is continuous and insatiable. The forms they send out are complex, cunning, and

It would be senseless to live in the country without a few hens pecking around the door

comprehensive. It is no trouble to tell the Department how many cows we have, and how many of these are pregnant; what stock of sows in pig, barren sows, and other sows roam around our domain; our count of old boars and young boars, stallions, gilts, rams kept for service, and members of the Women's Land Army. Promptly and with a sunny heart I fill in, again and again, the fullest details of all the combine harvesters that reap my couple of acres; my various tractors and broadcasting machines and manure spreaders. They forget nothing; although I can never give as much information as I would in answer to Item 94. My entry, '1', against 'Ducks, Geese and Turkeys of all ages' seems to me to tell them next to nothing.

It was not at the completing of another form or two that I hesitated, but at the time it takes to discover the right clerk with the right rubber stamp.

'It's a pity,' the saw-miller remarked, explaining the difficulties, 'that all those big packing-cases they send the tractors in from America are smashed up for firewood.'

At the railway station I saw several truck-loads of such cases, and being a man who takes a delight in working with wood, my mouth began to water. Thick, beautiful stuff it was; each box as big as a very sizable henhouse, and sturdy enough to contain a raging lion.

'It can't be true,' I asked a porter, 'that all this goes for firewood?'

'By order of the Ministry of Something-or-Other,' he nodded. 'They're sent to Dundee. To be broken up.'

'I can hardly bear it!'

'Aye, but worse than that. I'm told they're so full of nails, they're not worth the handling. I've heard there's dozens of them dumped in some old quarry, rotting.'

It happened that the Ministry of Something-or-Other relented just at that time, and I was lucky enough to be able to buy two of the huge packing-cases. They were about ten by six by five feet, and I was disappointed at first to see that each had been taken apart into its six component sections. The reason was soon obvious, and appreciated. It took one man, his wife, and two sturdy daughters all their time to turn a single section over, let alone lift it.

The outer boards, nearly an inch thick, were of beautiful planed pine. The interior of the boxes was lined with waterproof bitumen-coated paper, and braced with enough hefty battens to withstand a dozen shipwrecks.

The Americans are renowned for doing things in a big way, and they had excelled themselves over those cases. I should never accuse their maker of having been slipshod in one small respect. Rather do I like to believe that he, too, was a fellow who knew the satisfaction of possessing a few nice boards, even second-hand ones. He was too sound a craftsman to have made a mistake so simple, so silly, and so extensive and obvious. He must have done it on purpose, for the delight and convenience of such as I, who would one day set about undoing his handiwork.

This kindly Yankee, this better-than-a-brother, had chosen each one of his hundreds, his thousands of nails just half an inch longer than was necessary. Busily he had driven them in, rank upon rank of them—and not a single one of the protruding points had he turned down. They bristled all over the heavy sections, making them look like so many beds for cartoon fakirs. They put up no fight. They did not need to be assailed with screw-driver or pliers. A well-aimed tap with a hammer, and each bobbed in to present, on the other side, a head thrust out and waiting willingly for the same hammer's claws.

Claw-hammer? Ah, no!

Before we made another move towards the new henhouse we went to Dundee for hinges and lock, and in the ironmonger's a kindly Providence guided my wandering eye to a row of strong steel bars which hung from the edge of a high shelf. They had one end fashioned to wedge-shape; the other curved like walking-sticks—and fitted with nail-drawing claws.

'What are those?' I inquired.

The assistant knew my weakness. I cannot resist a new tool.

'Them?' said the well-meaning fellow. 'They're wrecker-bars. You wouldn't have much use for the like of that. We sell them mostly to shopkeepers—for opening up packing-cases.'

Instantly I became the owner of a steel wrecker-bar, and never did a few shillings bring a handsomer reward.

Alas, it was dusk when we got home, all eager to try the new tool. But there were fifty yards of electric cable kicking around, and it was a simple thing to fit a plug on one end and a lampholder on the other. Cheerfully I unfixed my bedside lamp and, armed with three hammers and two daughters, marched to the field where the wood lay.

The countryside rang with din. We all knelt on the points of nails, and got legs and hands horribly scratched, but we whacked away until we had beaten in the last spike on the first of those sides and we managed to turn it over.

Claw-hammer? A toy of a tool, compared with a wrecker-bar! It positively sucked those nails out, with a deliciously satisfying sound. We squabbled with each other, the daughters and I, about which should have the privilege of drawing them. In no time we had a good five pounds of nails collected in a bucket. The first side was separated into ten fine, even boards and a Union Jack of battens. We went indoors, mightily content, to do some geometry on the plans.

We sawed and hammered for a fortnight, the fall of dusk no handicap with our special lighting system. At the end of it we had a henhouse—and what a henhouse!—and over and above as fine a supply of surplus wood as the heart of handyman could desire.

The pitched roof gives ample headroom. The suite of five nesting-boxes with dome-shaped entrances are the finest thing of their kind in Perthshire. The long rectangular window, brainily placed at hen's-eye-level, is set in grooves and mounted on eight wooden wheels so that, in theory at least, it opens and closes at the merest touch.

We were delighted with our handiwork, and sorry when it was finished. With the light tied to the cross-bar of the central pair of couples we looked around the cosy interior when the last nail was driven, and in my pride and pleasure I let out a very careless remark.

'It looks almost too good for hens!'

The daughters' eyes lit up.

'Oh . . . could we, Daddy?'

'Could you what?'

'Put a good thick layer of straw on the floor—and sleep in it?'

They took up residence, and the hens went on roosting in the yews.

November arrived. The pullets were coming to an age when, if they were kindly treated, they ought to be starting to lay. The two usurpers were turned out of their home, and to make sure that Clucky's brood would be desperate with hunger in the morning and thus easy to manage, they were sent supperless to bed.

'We'll put their corn in the henhouse in the morning,' it was decreed. 'They'll walk in, and we'll lock the door. Simple!'

Simple! At the sight of the familiar food-basin they followed at heel like a pack of hounds. They watched the corn being tossed among the straw where Sally and Margie had slept. We drew back and waited for them to cross the threshold of the new abode.

Not a hen ventured in. Not one. And when we tried to drive them in, they fled in all directions.

Until that day they had been as tame a crowd of chickens as anyone could wish. They had been christened with individual names. They had eaten out of our hands. They had thought nothing of flocking indoors when they felt it was time for a snack. But when we tried to catch them, panic took them, and it was three days before we managed to round the last one up.

They were left for a fortnight to settle down in their ultra-comfortable quarters, with plenty of corn to scratch for on their well lit floor; copious fresh water; draught-free perches which they soon learned to use; every modern convenience.

We deliberately chose a day of villainous weather to let them out again. The meanest of all winds in these parts was blowing at thirty m.p.h.—a south-easter, laden with sleet. Watching from my study window during the afternoon as the bedraggled birds mooched dismally about, I was very glad to think of their having so cosy a house to retire to. Surely, soon, we would be rewarded with the first egg.

After tea I went to close their door. I looked at the perches. Empty! Every hen had gone back to the yew trees and, swaying and soaked, was riding out the gale.

There, in spite of all our efforts to reconcile them to the sweetness of civilization, they insisted on remaining. We had to give up trying in the end, and leave them to their own choice.

'It simply means they're not worth keeping,' I said. 'We'll see no eggs till March, at the earliest.'

But well before Christmas they were laying like fury. From then on, winter and summer, we have had eggs galore—and, always, an empty henhouse.

Of all the creatures I have to feed every day, I like none better than the poultry, and therefore they are no tie. As for the mess they make—certainly, in spring, they do the daffodils no good with their scraping, and at moulting-time their scattered feathers look a trifle unsightly until a good wind carries them away. But brown feathers blowing about look not much different from brown leaves, which are with us the year through.

On that score, the daughters now are dissatisfied that we did not go in for a pure white breed.

It is not that they are specially fond of untidiness; still less are they fond of tidying up. But they have heard of a lady who keeps the grounds of her house very spick and span, and who was embarrassed when a friend presented her with a dozen white Leghorn pullets.

It was a gift which could not be refused; indeed, it would have been warmly welcomed but for the thought of how the well kept lawn would look when they began to moult.

Then she had an idea. She dyed them green!

CHAPTER NINE

KIRSCHEN AND TONTO

EVERY life holds moments which glow with so clear a brilliance that the memory of them goes on shining for years. They do not always bear analysis. Taken apart, their contents can seem incongruous. The component which really matters is never there to be examined again. It is the mood of the hour.

Sometimes a symbol can remain to re-light the lamp of recollection, and for my wife and myself such a one is that standing joke of the canine world—that animated sausage, half a dog high and a dog-and-a-half long, the comical dachshund.

Our children have grown up with the feeling that of all the breeds of dog, something belongs to the dachshund which is special and unique. They still find it hard to believe that this viewpoint of theirs arises from something which does not concern them in the least.

Mary and I spent our honeymoon motoring in Germany. In the course of our tour we drove down the valley of the River Moselle, and came to the little town of Cochem. There, high above the grey roofs and the blue water, stands yet another ancient *schloss*. We climbed up a steep track between the vineyards to have a look at it.

The day was drenched in sunlight. Ox-carts ambled lazily among the vines. Cherries hung ripe on the trees, and here and there along the dusty roads rosy-faced fraus and tow-headed children held out bagfuls for passing motorists to stop and buy.

'*Kirschen! Kirschen!*'

We stopped, and bought.

The river flowed placidly through its great valley. Brown-skinned men and girls, as nearly naked as they dared, rowed upstream and down, singing as they went. We had lunched at an ancient country inn from whose cellar mine host had brought a great jug of sharp, cool Moselle wine straight from the wood. Life was as nearly perfect for two people as life can ever be.

No one was about, up at the *schloss*. We wandered in and around it, looking at its antique stones, but looking still oftener at that glorious scene. Presently there was a pattering, and from somewhere two dogs appeared: a pair of long-haired golden dachshunds.

They were as friendly a couple of characters as we have ever come across. They gave us as ready a welcome as most of the natives had done. The sun shone on their beautifully kept hair as we persuaded them to pose for a photograph, and ever since then the sight or even the name of a golden dax. has set the wine flowing from the wood again, and the cherries shining fatly in the trees, and the sweating labourers smiling an open-faced greeting.

This honeymoon memory is surely our own affair. But for years the daughters kept bringing out that snapshot from Cochem, and—

'Oh, Daddy, I do wish we had a dachshund . . .'

One day when they said it, and when their words had bounced as easily as usual off this resistant hide, their mother gave a small sigh and made a confession:

'I've wanted one too—ever since Cochem.'

'Not more pets! Heavens, not more!' cried the bridegroom of that idyllic scene . . . and forthwith, in great secrecy, began making inquiries, and discovered with some awe that the price of a well bred pup was likely to be anywhere in the region of fifteen guineas.

Around the same time Sally thrust a newspaper at me, pointing to an advertisement:

'Dachshund, free to good home . . .'

That, thought I, might be more in the line of a good Aberdonian. We set off to see it, not daring to imagine that we would be the first to go snatching at such a chance.

The man was at home. He greeted us genially. No one else had got in ahead of us. Courteously but carefully he questioned us, making sure that we were the sort of people who would give the best possible care to his pet.

We told him of all our other livestock; of lives spent doing little else but caring for an assortment of animals and birds. He was impressed. He nodded.

'I think I'd like you to have him,' he said, 'but he'll have to say the final word himself. I'll let him out, and we'll see if he takes to you.'

He went to a shed at the back of the cottage. There was a merry barking, and round the corner romped the dachshund, to leap up in turn at Sally and Margie; to lick Mary's hands; to caper about them and roll at their feet in an ecstasy of instant friendship. Margie, then aged seven, was entirely captivated. But Sally, who was twelve, looked up uncertainly as she patted the affectionate creature.

'I didn't know,' she said, 'that there were black-and-white dachshunds.'

Nor did I.

His colouring was in large irregular patches, very artistically splashed on. He was, in his way, an attractive beast. But . . .

'Is he pure-bred?' I asked his owner.

'Oh, yes! Pure!'

'You . . . er . . . know the parents?'

'I have his mother. She has won prizes. Pure—yes.'

'And the sire?'

'A prize-winner too. Pure—oh, certainly. He was a pure-bred fox terrier.'

Somehow the daughters were lured into the car minus the black-and-white dachshund.

'Daddy, you'll just have to get one now!'

'At fifteen guineas? An Aberdonian like me?'

They sighed. That was nothing. But their mother sighed too . . .

The Victorian paterfamilias must have had the time of his life, blustering around the home and bellowing in a harsh, dictatorial voice. I tried it once, and enjoyed it thoroughly; none the less so because it was the one and only time I have ever succeeded in reducing a certain Cockney to tears.

The storm blew up over no more important a thing than a square wooden box, for which the sum of one shilling had been added to an account.

'What's happened,' I demanded, 'to that crate the new tea-set came in a while ago? I haven't seen it since it was unpacked.'

'The crate? Oh—I've stored a lot of old tea-plates in it, and saucers and things, from broken sets.'

'In heaven's name, what use will a lot of old saucers and plates ever be to you? They're only junk! Tipple them out! Set them up and let the children throw stones at them! Cluttering the place up with rubbish! Get rid of them!'

'But . . .'

'Now! Right away! I want it now!'

'What . . .'

'Look it out. Empty it. Measure it. Cut up some old material. Make a cushion to fit it.'

'How . . .'

'For your golden dachshund. It's arriving today.'

And so, astonishingly, tears—not, indeed, for the play-acting, which had been too crude to be taken seriously, but for a sudden shock of pleasure which had not been quite anticipated. A rare moment, and linked up, of course, with crimson cherries and amber wine and blue water under sparkling sunlight.

The new puppy was coming from Weymouth; almost as long a journey as it could have made to us, starting on the British mainland. There were to be several changes of train, and in the dead of winter at that.

'Don't count on it too much,' I pleaded, still startled by those delighted tears, 'until you see it here alive and kicking. They're delicate little things—and you know what railway people are.'

That was a gross slander. In this country place we are accustomed to kindly, old-fashioned country service, and none give it more graciously than the station staff. But at Bristol? At Birmingham? At Rugby or Crewe or Perth, or wherever the pup had to be moved from one train to another?

'If it gets here alive, it'll be a miracle,' I said.

She got here alive. If she had been under personal escort all the way she could not have arrived a second sooner. Somewhere on the journey the parcel of food tied to her travelling box had disappeared; the little dachshund's waistline told where it had gone. Her dish had been filled with fresh water, and how many guards and porters, unknown and untipped and unthanked, had helped her on her way—that we did not know. When she arrived at Wester Denhead from Weymouth, something like six hundred miles by rail, she was as fit as if she had come from next door. So, in this household, no more slanders on railwaymen, but only hats off.

'You go alone and fetch her,' I told Mary. 'Take her out of the box and make a fuss of her. Then she'll know from the start that she's yours.'

In the dog line we had never possessed anything so small as a dachshund. We were accustomed to rough-and-tumble shooting dogs, not lapdogs. Mary spent the first half-hour alone with the dax. before I went through to the lounge to inspect the new arrival.

'Pet her,' I had said. 'Coddle her. Coming after that miserable journey, she'll never forget it.'

No petting was going on. No fussing and no coddling. My wife was sitting with a bewildered look while a sturdy pup with tiny, twinkling legs marched round and round and round the room, the small pads making a surprisingly loud thumping on the carpet.

'You're not fondling her,' I remarked.

'She won't let me! She just squirms out of my arms. That's all she'll do—march round the floor.'

We looked at the delicately bred pup which had just ended a trying trip from the south coast of England to snow-bound Perthshire, and for which so many careful preparations had been made. There was nothing weak or fragile in the set of that resolute jib. No lion ever paced its cage with more dignity or more indifference. Quite plainly she was out to walk all the way back to Weymouth, independent alike of our coddling and of the good nature of the railway staff.

We called Judy in. She looked in amazement at this new phenomenon; sniffed at it, and seemed hardly able to believe that it could be dog. I couldn't resist saying:

'Fetch it here!'

Judy did her best to retrieve it. But it slipped out of her grasp and went on walking.

With occasional stops for rest and refreshment it walked for the better part of three days, but at last it seemed to feel that it had arrived. Judy, who had followed it around until she was dizzy, flung herself down on the rug exhausted. The pup curled up between her legs, and fell into a deep sleep. The two have been the most devoted of friends ever since.

Remembering those cherries, we called her Kirschen.

Everyone who has ever owned more than one must know that dogs have almost as much individuality of character as human beings. It cannot possibly be true, as is sometimes said, that their nature reflects their masters'. If it were, I should certainly be a many-sided person!

Danny was lonely hearted and anxious to please. Old Gippy was an individualist, with a certain sardonic malice and a permanently bad conscience. We have had Nell, timid and sensitive; Meg, who kept aloof; and others stupid or benign, light-headed or cunning or servile. We have never had a ferocious dog; nothing even remotely equalling Colonel Honky for venom. If such a one found its way among us, it would not stay for long.

Of them all, we have never kept a pleasanter one than Judy. Her nature is sunshine through and through. She fears nothing, never cringes, and offers an open-hearted welcome to everyone. She wants to take part in every activity of every member of the family, from leaping for treacly buns with the children at Hallowe'en to lying contentedly for hours on the path as I work in the garden. Nothing disturbs her. Nothing angers her.

Kirschen is different again, and since dachshunds are little known compared with the spaniels, the terriers, and the labs, it might be of interest to other dog-lovers to give a character sketch of the breed. There are several good reasons why their popularity is increasing.

This grim, three-day walk of Kirschen's when she first arrived was, as it turned out, a token of a highly independent nature. She is as self-contained as any cat, and far less fond of being petted. She has a habit of slipping away from the caressing hand, to sit just far enough from the fire to save her whiskers from singeing.

Yet she is very affectionate, especially towards the children. She watches for them coming home from school, and when they arrive those stout-muscled little legs send her leaping a yard in the air again and again in an ecstasy of welcome. She lets them haul and maul at her, dress her up and wheel her about, with astonishing complacency.

As for dachshunds being lapdogs—heavens, we soon learned differently! It is true that she likes to sit on a lap—the female variety greatly preferred—and to lounge on silken cushions. Indoors she is as dainty, as luxury-loving, and as charming as any of the small breeds, but that is only one side of her character.

The Kennel Club lists dachshunds among the sporting varieties, and the Kennel Club was never so right. They may be short in the limb, but they are still man-size hounds, as I proved the first time she sneaked after Judy and me on a shooting expedition. She had had no training. She was a complete stranger to game of any kind. But she worked her way through the prickliest rough with complete indifference to the comfort of her own hide, and she put out as much game as did Judy. Now, the instant she sees the gun being lifted, she is at the door, ready, tying herself in knots with excitement—and however much my neighbours may laugh at me, I don't leave her behind. Except for one thing, she is a top-notch little gun-dog with a nose as good as any spaniel's. She covers her ground busily and thoroughly, and she is remarkably steady.

The one lack is that she has not the slightest interest in fallen game, which she will pass by with scarcely a sniff.

If any family man who happens to read these pages should be thinking of buying a pup for his wife and children; a handy-sized beast which will not take up the whole of the hearth-rug; a good-tempered creature that will bear with any amount of attention, and yet a dog which he himself can take out after rats or rabbits and see a bit of sport—a dachshund is the animal.

And should this advice be accepted, I can only hope that any others who may be lured to prove the endearing qualities of the breed will not have half the difficulty we experienced in house-training Kirschen.

Judy, who, on a careful count, once made twenty-nine pools in the house on a single day, was soon taught good manners. With Kirschen, we thought the time-honoured methods would never have any success. We did manage it in the end, but it is only fair to confess that even when she was seven months old, and had had countless lessons, the most she had learned was to use the bathroom—and then scoot out of doors as fast as her legs would carry her!

At Cochem on the Moselle there had been two. At Wester Denhead there was only one. She was, and is, the property of the mistress of the house, although at least half her affection is for daughter Margie. Almost certainly, in her own mind, Kirschen is Margie's dog. But she is not that in fact, and so:

'Oh, Daddy, I wish I had a dachshund *of my own* . . .'

Therefore, when Kirschen was eighteen months old, new inquiries were set afoot, and an address in Ayrshire was discovered. Stud fee, five guineas. Oh, Scotland! Oh, canny Aberdeen!

Margie named her one Kleine; named it even before Miss K. had set off on her nuptial journey to the land of Robbie Burns.

She had the time of her life, had Mrs K., when she came back from her five-guinea mating. She was given a raw fresh egg with her supper. She was given milk, and a cut off the joint. A special trip was made to the chemist's for an outsize bottle of cod-liver oil and malt extract. That disgusting stuff, said to

Dainty, luxury-loving . . . but that is only one side of her character

be so good for children, is shuddered at by ours. We had discovered quite by accident, trying Judy with an experimental spoonful from an unwanted jar, that she would fairly gobble it. Now, nothing will make her and Kirschen lick their chops so eagerly as the sight of the rubbery mess, and Mrs K. had as much of it as she wanted from then on.

'Kleine! Kleine!' Margie called about the house, practising.

She learned to spell it. She learned to write it in German script. She got a collar and a lead, a basket and a cushion, a dainty, Kleine-sized dish.

The weeks passed very slowly. Kirschen lived on the fat of the land—and yet, in her own person, never seemed to grow noticeably fatter.

The great day dawned, but of course we had had more than suspicions before then.

Five guineas, forsooth! And not a sausage!

About a year before we acquired Kirschen, a man who was then a stranger to us bought a donkey for his son, and some time afterwards, quite unexpectedly, this donkey produced a foal. The daughters had news of the happy event almost as soon as it had taken place, and:

'Oh, Daddy, a baby donkey! I wish . . .'

'No! No! No!'

'But couldn't we just go and see it?'

'No! No!'

Coupar Angus prides itself, and justly, on holding one of the finest annual horse shows in Britain. In few places, if anywhere, can a better display of animals and decorated harness be seen. In our household it is talked of for weeks in advance, and on the great day itself the daughters vanish in the early morning and are missing until nightfall.

That year, I stayed away from it. Grimly, deliberately. There was a special attraction which I was resolved not to see. The baby donkey was to be on view.

Mary was lured to the show with her sketch-book, and although the curiosity of the crowd became too much for her before she had got down more than a few lines, that page was thrust at me at least a hundred times during the following year.

One day I was strolling innocently home from posting a letter when a car pulled up beside me, and there was my friend the vet.

'Ah, Jimmie, I've been looking for you. You don't by any chance happen to want a year-old donkey?'

'I couldn't want anything less!'

'It struck me it might be just the thing for Sally and Margaret. There's a client of mine who bought a donkey for his boy, and it had a foal. He wants a good home for it . . .'

'Bill, every day I have to feed mice, rabbits, pet ducks, guinea-pigs, hens, bantams, pigeons, canaries, dogs, an ill-tempered monster of a gander, and boxes upon boxes of caterpillars. For heaven's sake, don't let my children know that there's any possibility of them getting hold of that donkey!'

Arriving home late for lunch, I explained the reason to Mary, not knowing that the daughters were within earshot. Two hours later we were off to see the cuddy.

We named him Tonto. He arrived on a large livestock lorry. He was too young to be ridden. He was, so far as I could see, of no use whatever. But he was pretty, and tame, and friendly, and he submitted placidly to being put on a rope and led on a one-mile-an-hour walk round and round the field. The daughters were charmed.

'What's to happen in the winter?' I demanded. 'We have no stable.'

'It's a long, long time to winter . . .'

Long or short, it began to arrive—but not before Tonto was as firmly established as Honky or any of the others. There could be no question of getting rid of him. He was one of the family.

On cold, wet nights we worried about him, wondering where we could find him house-room. Some people assured us that a donkey should be hardy enough to stay out in the worst of weather, but by voice and manner he told us that he did not like it. Not even a wet hen could look more miserable than he when he was drenched.

After one specially stormy night I went out to give him a ration of bruised oats. He was nowhere to be seen. The field was empty. I glanced around the hedges, remembering without much assurance the extraordinary old belief that no one ever sees a dead donkey.

From beyond the semicircle of fencing which cuts off one small section of the field I heard a snickering bray. Behind that fence is our carefully built hen-house, for which the hens had shown so much contempt. From the doorway looked Tonto, contented and dry, very little the worse for his argument with the barbed wire. He had found a stable for himself. We other donkeys had never thought of it.

In contrast to Kirschen, he needed no training to be house-clean. He is free to go and come as he likes, and we have found that he is quite fastidious in his habits. He has chosen one inconspicuous spot in the field as his bathroom, and thither he goes, every time.

Once a week I march down with the wheelbarrow and carry a very handy load to the garden. Even junior donkeys have their uses!

CHAPTER TEN

IT'S CATCHING

NO man lives for long in the country without discovering that it is overcrowded. For his own comfort he has to learn the rudiments of the art and craft of catching things. This can, at times, have its sporting qualities, but in the main it is an urgent necessity.

Rats are the arch-enemies. I cannot recollect anyone ever having said a good word for them, although there was one, once, for which we came to feel a kind of half-reluctant admiration.

He was half-grown, a sleek and healthy-looking fellow, and he discovered the bird table by the kitchen window. He would come helping himself under our very noses, not snatching a bit and bolting with it, but sitting up eating impudently as we watched. I dared not shoot him in case a ricocheting bullet should smash the glass, and a gin trap was almost certain to kill a bird.

We bought a cage trap, one whole end of which was a door which could be set open, with a cunning arrangement of spring, hook, and platform for snapping it shut. There was a second, slanting door at the other end, reached by a small corridor and held down by its own weight. The theory was that when one rat

120

had used the main entrance and it had banged behind him, others would push their way in through this back door.

We baited the platform with bread and the hook with bacon, and put the trap on the bird table.

'If a greenfinch goes in,' said Margie, 'can we keep it for a pet?'

Greenfinches, taken from the wild, make engaging company. But it was rats we were after.

As it happened, although we had many birds so tame that they came tapping at the window for a snack, not one ventured inside the trap. If simple-minded birds were so suspicious of it, there seemed little chance of capturing the wily rat.

He arrived quite soon, and we watched him start back in surprise at the sight of this unusual object in his dining room. He inspected it warily; walked around it; sniffed at its appetizing smells, and made off. But in a very short time he was back again, curious, cautious, but tempted. Over a couple of hours he made a dozen visits, and at last he crossed the threshold. The bacon had done it. He took a tentative tug at the tempting rasher and—snap! We had him.

The thing to do then was to sink the trap in the rain-water barrel for a few minutes. We had seen all there was to see of a rat catching himself in a wire cage, and even those detestable pests deserve the kindness of a quick dispatch once they are cornered.

But there was the question of this intriguing little back door, and the doubt whether it was always the same rat we had been seeing, or one of a litter. We decided to let him stay awhile, and we kept an eye open for some of his relations to come and join him. None did, but we had a very interesting view of that classic symbol of cowardice, the trapped rat. He caused us to revise some of our ideas.

He could see us, of course, on the other side of the window. He knew the plight he was in, but there was nothing of the craven about him. True enough, a rat will squeal in terror as some murderous weapon swings down on him. But so will a man.

No, this one did not waste time wailing to high heaven about his terror. Single-mindedly he set about the job of getting out again. He ran about the cage, testing the wires here and there with his teeth. We noticed for the first time, almost sentimentally, how dainty and delicate are a rat's hands. They were clean and pinkish and pretty little four-fingered hands, almost like miniature human ones as they grasped at the wires.

'Poor thing . . .' said Margie.

He was a rat in a hurry, but never, we believed, in a panic. His actions were too methodical for that. He bit here, and bit there, feeling out those wires, but he never bit in the same place twice—until he came to one spot, up towards a corner. Was there a flaw in the metal at that point? Or had he decided, simply, that the wise thing to do was to concentrate his energy on the one place? He worked away for half an hour, and

'He's done it!'

'Impossible,' I said.

But there it was—one of the bars was severed. He braced himself with hands and feet. He pushed with his nose. Exerting prodigies of strength he got the broken wire to bend. He had his head through. He dragged and squeezed and pushed with his plump body, and even if he was only a rat, and was more truly caught than ever when he had stuck half-way, we did not go out with a stick to finish him off.

He managed it, and as he flashed out of sight in the herbaceous border we were all of one mind.

'He deserves to get away!'

Nothing so spoils the spirit of warfare as getting to know your enemy too well.

The same cage trap, which is not nearly so effective as a common gin, figured in another incident in which I was paid a very doubtful compliment.

A rat had found its way into the house. My wife set the cage in the bathroom, where a hole by one of the water pipes had been enlarged. Cheese, bread, bacon, suet, grain, and dripping—night after night she tried a variety of baits, but the visitor was having none of them. Then I noticed that a pile of manuscript duplicates in the study seemed to be diminishing. The carbon copy of a short story was discovered, mysteriously, under the bath.

'The rats must be taking them,' said Mary, and screwed up a few pages of fiction and tossed them into the trap. The next morning, she had the rat.

This business of rat-catching is surrounded by a good deal of ballyhoo. Your professional likes to put it around that there are mysteries and secrets in it; that Mr Rat is as wise and wily as the devil himself, gifted with an uncanny intelligence and not to be lured to his doom except by a cunning which is the special possession of those who have made a lifetime study of the rodent mind.

Rubbish! They have very little intelligence, and not nearly so much suspicion as is generally made out. I used to take the greatest care to hide my traps under sawdust or sand or chaff, to wear gloves while I was setting them to keep the smell of my hands from them, and a lot of troublesome nonsense like that. As often as not the trap got clogged with the covering material, and failed to go off.

Now, never bothering with gloves, I set the trap down bare and unconcealed in some narrow passage where a rat is likely to run. He walks into it every time.

The record—and none of your professionals can hope to beat it—was made on a day when Judy told me that there was a rat in the wood-pile. As she barked and tried to push her nose between the logs I got a gin out. I was still bent over it, having just finished setting it and not yet put it in place, when Judy got the rat to bolt. It darted between my legs—clean into the trap.

But periodically, especially when some one has been threshing or tidying up nearby, we suffer such an invasion that the only answer is poison.

That is easy enough too, where there are no other animals about. They will take poison, especially one of the kinds with a phosphorous content, as readily as they will take poultry food. The snag is that they will persist in carrying it about and dropping pieces here and there. Then—a dead hen, a dead dog or rabbit, even, unthinkably, a gander cut off at the beginning of his allotted half-century.

There is red squill, which is harmful only to rodents. Rats will not gobble it so greedily as some other concoctions, but if care is taken to clear up anything else they might eat, they will take baits impregnated with it.

One such raid, one spring, sent me off for a bottle of liquid red squill. The chemist looked at me in surprise when I asked for it.

'I haven't seen any in years! The Agricultural Executive Committee—or somebody—gets it all nowadays.'

'Well, I'm risking nothing else,' said I. 'I'd rather have the rats. What do they do with it all?'

'I suppose they issue it to the professional catchers.'

Not knowing one, I prepared to do the best possible without. But it happened that exactly two days later a very dapper stranger wearing a smart black 'Anthony Eden' hat, and carrying on his back a bulky game-bag, called at Wester Denhead. He announced that he was a rat-catcher. He opened up his bag. It was packed with liquid red squill; bottle upon bottle of it; gallons of it.

He was full of knowledgeable talk about rats.

'D'you know why they die with red squill, and other beasts don't? Because a rat's so made that it can't vomit.'

'D'you know why they breed so fast? Because they have two wombs, and as soon as one litter is born there's another on the way.'

He was, I gathered, a veritable Pied Piper among rat-catchers. He understood all the mysteries and all the secrets. Only certain people were endowed with the gift. He made an inspection of Wester Denhead, and guaranteed that he would rid the place of the last and final rat for four pounds.

Indelicately I suggested that if he would sell me the smallest of his bottles I could do the job for myself. But no! But no! The precious stuff had to be used to the best advantage by skilled hands.

We settled for two pounds, one to be paid on the spot, and the other when the miracle was accomplished to my complete satisfaction. I handed over a note, and he said he would go at once and get some materials. In the garage he eyed my bicycle. It was a pity to waste time walking . . .

I frowned. It was a good bicycle. I had a use for it.

'I'll leave my bag,' he said. 'I'll not be gone for more than half an hour.'

Off he set on my cycle. For months afterwards, as I trudged into Coupar Angus to post a letter or buy an evening paper, I was grinningly greeted by one and another of my country friends:

'No' bikin' the nicht, Mr Young?'

Lacking a bike, I haven't been able to go bikin' ever since.

If I lost my cycle, and if I was too cautious to try out the brownish potion in the many bottles which the expert had left behind, the transaction was not all loss. The world and his wife, sharing the joke of the Aberdonian who had been 'done', became aware of my rat problem, and hurried, in the generous way of country folk, to offer advice. There were, I discovered, countless ways of getting rid of rats.

For instance, one worthy mentioned that it was only necessary to catch a single one alive, soak it in paraffin, set it alight, and let it run. All the others would get such a fright that they would leave the place.

No doubt! Some of our rat population make their home under the foundations of the house. They would have been well away before it fell blazing about their ears.

There was another idea, on slightly similar lines. Again we had to catch one; this time a big, strong, old male. It had to be starved for several days—just that—and then released.

'It'll be so hungry, it'll turn cannibal,' we were told. 'It'll start killing the rest of your rats right and left—they'll clear out and go elsewhere to get away from it.'

And then? Would it follow up the fugitives? Or, having cultivated a taste for hot red blood, would it turn and sample the other inhabitants of the house? We did not risk making the test.

'Try ratlime!' one friend offered.

We tried it. We smeared the filthy, sticky mess on a piece of wood, cut to fit exactly between the wall and an open door in a passage. A rat had made a hole there, and we decided that it could not possibly get into the house without crossing the treacherous board.

It couldn't and didn't. It was caught the first night. In the morning, still floundering weakly and able to draw in wheezy breaths through the one corner of one nostril which was not clogged with the villainous stuff, it presented so revolting a spectacle that we found ourselves being sorry even for a rat. Floor and door and wall were plastered with the lime. It took months to get the last of it off.

We did not use ratlime again—for rats. But at a time when flypapers could not be bought we thought of smearing some thinly on strips of wood and hanging them in the kitchen. They were deadly. We rid ourselves of flies—and, watching the invention working, the quaint thought struck me that odd things might happen if a bearded sailor, and the girl he was quarrelling with, and one of these patent fly-catchers, all got mixed up together. The story, called 'Permission To Grow', may, where it appeared, have amused some of my present readers.

There was still another idea which we had a notion to try. It was said to have come originally from China.

The equipment needed was a barrel and a piece of stiff, springy parchment. The barrel was to be half filled with water, and a small block of wood set afloat in it. Then the top was to be covered with the stretched parchment, firmly tied, and some grain was to be laid on that. A plank was to be leant casually against the barrel, to make it easy for the rats to get up.

For a few nights they were to be fed on the parchment table, until they were sure of it. After about a week—a razor blade, and a neat cross cut in the centre.

Along comes the first rat. The cut parchment yields. In he slides. The parchment flips back into position.

A rat is able to swim around for only a very short time, and then it drowns. That is why the thoughtful Chinese put the square of wood in the water. Victim Number One finds it; climbs up on it; shakes himself, and sets about planning how he can get out of this mess.

Along comes the second rat. Splash! Swimming for dear life, it sees its brother high and dry on the wooden block. It tries to get up. But the cunning

Chinese provide only a one-seater rescue raft. There is no room for two. As one gets on, the other tumbles off. They start to fight. They squeal and swear.

Rats, so the Chinese say, are insatiable fight-fans. Wherever there is a battle among their kind there they must be, either to watch or to take part. The din of this struggle to the death draws every other rat on the premises to the top of the barrel. In they plop, one by one, to argue it out for possession of the one-rat raft, and in the morning all are drowned but the sole survivor who, triumphantly perched on the block, has only to be tippled off and there you are once again rid of your enemies.

I have the barrel, and when I can lay my hands on a suitable piece of parch-ment I mean to put this method to the test. The only reason why I did not go ahead with it immediately after the loss of my bicycle gained me so much informa-tion was that, searching for something else on a shelf of the tool shed, I came upon an almost full bottle of red squill. I used it, and was left with no rats for the experiment.

Then there are moles. Maddening, they are, in the garden. Invariably the routes they choose for their tunnels are directly under the drills of growing vege-tables. They follow them up and down, as if for nothing but deliberate malice. Of course, under the drills is dung, and among the dung are the finest and fattest worms. Wild nature can often be a nuisance, but it is not given to playing mean tricks.

After many pokings with bamboo canes we discovered one of their main entrances to the garden, and since then the trouble has been easy to check.

From the kitchen comes the call: 'There's a mole working.' I nip out, go quietly to a certain spot, slip a tunnel-type trap into their run, and then go clump-ing round the path. The invisible mole takes fright at the heavy footsteps and makes for quieter surroundings. I wait for a couple of minutes, and I have him.

We busied ourselves, at one time, skinning them, and a very tidy job we made of it, pinning row upon row of them out on a board, each pelt complete from nose to tail. But we never managed to make a moleskin coat, nor even a pair of gloves. When we took a friend to admire our collection of skins, we found that skins were all we had. The moths had got at them. Every hair was gone.

Moles—and cats. However troublesome it may be at times, one does not destroy a neighbour's pet pussy. Usually a few encounters with Judy are enough to send it mooching elsewhere.

It was different when some stray from the town had a litter of kittens in the

She wants to take part

127

black shed by the edge of one of the raspberry fields. Four of them grew up and, having no kindly hand to supply the comforting saucer of milk or the odd cod's head, they picked up a living as best they could from the land.

A covey of small partridges in which I was taking a friendly interest began to shrink. Here and there fledgelings vanished from nests we had discovered. Snared rabbits were torn and destroyed.

Twice, out with the gun, Grandad got a chance. I myself bagged the third. The fourth, not knowing, came and attached itself to our premises; and not without encouragement from some members of the family. Going out in the darkness to lock up for the night, I would find myself stumbling over unexpected dishes of milk.

We are fond enough of cats, but they do too much damage among the birds. The order went out that this one was not to be fed—but still he came, and several times he was seen among the tangle at the bottom of the hedge, the tip of his tail twitching as he watched the chickens pecking about.

When Judy went after him he fled up a tree. He did that several times, refusing to be discouraged. He was a beauty; a grand, fat, grey cat with a splendid thick coat, a handsome head, and a particularly bushy tail. He would have been a fine ornament for any household, only that, having been reared to the joys of the wild, he would very rarely have been found at home.

I shot him, and as he fell from the tree I shouted Judy back to heel, in case his last act might be to scratch her eyes out.

Margie rushed to inquire about the bang, and looked very solemnly at the corpse.

'It's a pity,' she said, biting her lip.

I explained just why he had had to go. He would certainly have had a chicken or two. From chickens he might have graduated to bantams.

'You understand, don't you?' I said.

She was thoughtful for a moment more, and then:

'May I have his tail?'

So I chopped off the tail for her, and as she fondled it she remembered something.

'Daddy! You know that man who came—the one who was speaking about apples. He said that when a tree wasn't doing well, you should bury a cat among the roots.'

Forthwith we dug a useful hole under our biggest apple-tree; one which produces excellent, long-keeping fruit, but which until then had not given us

9

more than fourteen pounds in any season. We administered the prescribed tonic: one dead cat. Very interestedly we watched for the result. The following year that tree produced a bumper crop.

But so did all the others.

On the subject of cats which go a-hunting, and remembering Aunt Mary's fur rug, it might do no harm to pass on a tip which I was once given for ensuring that Puss should stay at home.

'The one thing they can't stand,' my old gamekeeper friend told me, 'is wet inside their ears. Cut their ears off and they'll never go far from home, in case they're caught in a shower.'

As we are not likely to change our views about keeping a cat, we shall not be faced with the problem of whether or not we are hardy enough to set upon it and prune it.

I snare and trap rabbits in full awareness that it involves more cruelty than anything else I do. It is necessary, but there is no pleasure in it.

There are only two ways of killing rabbits for which I confess a frank liking. The one is shooting them as they weave and flash among heavy cover; as good a sport as any landowner ever enjoys among his flocks of driven birds. The other it utterly primitive, but it can make the skin prickle with delicious excitement. It is to search for them as they lie couched in the long summer grass on a fine afternoon and, creeping up like any beast of prey, to plant a foot on the hindmost leg just as they bolt. Not once in twenty times does one get near enough to make a capture, but when it comes off—hang civilization! It's a thrill!

There is still another way of catching rabbits which we have yet to try, and which could easily be put into practice within twenty yards of our front door.

A rectangular pit is dug on some dry, sloping bank; say four feet long and two wide and two deep. Bottom and sides are lined with bricks or stout wood, and a few four-inch drainage tiles are inserted round the sides, their far ends blocked with slates.

From the two lower corners of the pit, two lengths of drain are laid, extending about eight or ten feet from the man-made burrow. These are the entrance holes. The pit is cosily lined with hay or straw, and a close-fitting lid is put over it and concealed under a scattering of earth or a few turves.

Wild rabbits, so it is said, will soon discover this comfortable pre-fab and take up residence. All that one has to do then is to go and poke a long stick up the two entrance holes. The alarmed inhabitants will scurry for safety into the tiles in the sides which, with the slates preventing further digging, will be just long enough to give a rabbit a sense of security without letting it get out of reach.

All that has to be done then, is to raise the lid and lift out your dinner.

About the pastime of catching things, which has a curious charm, I have picked up certain pieces of quite useless information.

Grandad, who can remember the days when sparrows were taken and sold at a few pence a dozen for the sport of some so-called shooting men, once talked to the children about a cunning contrivance which he named a skeevan. It may not be spelt in that way. The word, which he brought from Devon, is in no dictionary I have seen.

The skeevan is a pyramid-shaped cage with a tiny door at the top for taking out the captives. It is set by being propped on edge by a small twig. This twig is in contact with a length of supple branch which, bent to a half-circle, curves inwards from two corners of the cage.

Some crumbs are put down under it. Birds hop in, and at first they come to no harm. More gather to the feast, and they are pecking away busily when one of them notices the inviting bow above its head. An irresistible perch! When something even as small as a blue-tit alights on it, down falls the cage and imprisons the lot.

Plagued by the children, Grandad laboured skilfully and made them an excellent skeevan. It was tested, and it worked very efficiently. Whoever invented it was a bird psychologist, and knew they could not bear to see a perch without hopping on to it. We caught birds with the greatest of ease. But it was wasted labour, for we took them only to let them fly away again. We did not even trouble to wring the necks of the sparrows amongst them.

The same brace of daughters came home one day with the secret of how to catch wood-lice. All that had to be done was to hollow out a turnip and put it down in a suitable place. The insects would be found crowded inside it in the morning—dozens of them.

We hollowed a turnip and they placed it near the wood-pile; but, as we had never been troubled by wood-lice, we caught none. A grinning face was cut in the wasted turnip, and it was turned into a lantern.

And snails—periodically the children used to make an expedition to a nearby lane in whose shade, at certain seasons, brightly-shelled snails go foraging. They would bring back a tinful which climbed slimily over everything until even Mary lost patience and turned them out.

Finally that sport was strictly forbidden, and a very short time afterwards two splendid snails were discovered making their way around the rim of the kitchen sink. I had to spring to the defence of the daughters. I had brought these in myself—in the crop of a pheasant which had hung in the larder for over a week. They had hardly been set free when their horns were out and they were off at the gallop.

Some things are caught, and some others it seems better to leave to their freedom.

Up in Glenshee, on a sunny afternoon, we were picnicking by the river when the nearest thing to a fairy that any of us will ever see came fluttering over our heads, darting and planing, turning and skimming, against the peaceful sky.

It was a creature of the air, and hardly of the earth; in colour milky-white, flashing and shimmering in the sunlight. Its movements were a poem of lightness and grace. The ethereal beauty of it was something to wonder at. It was a pure albino sand-martin.

We had it to ourselves for an hour, but presently our peace was invaded. A group of twenty-odd cyclists swung down the track sign-posted 'Dangerous Ford' and, leaning their machines against the dike, set about gathering wood to make a fire.

One after another, they spotted the fairy-like white bird. They were city boys, but quite evidently they felt as much surprise and pleasure at the sight of it as we had. So charmed, they were, that . . . they wanted it. They had to have it down out of the sky.

A party of them set off for the sandbank to which, every so often, the white martin was going with its catch of flies. Several times it darted into its hole, and was all but captured as it came out.

It stopped going to its nest. It stayed in the air. So the boys—meaning, most likely, no harm—took the only other way they could think of to get possession of it. They began to throw stones at it.

We hurried on our way, leaving them to their sport. We went back to the same spot the following year, and watched the sand-martins flying. There was no sign of a white one amongst them.

To dogs, of course, the height of pleasure lies in the catching of living things. A gun-dog learns to discriminate and mostly pays attention only to game, but old Danny, in his day, had a great fancy for hedgehogs.

I have told already, in *The Blue Bowl*, of how he used to bring them to me, his mouth bleeding, and how, rather than offend him, I would let him drop them into my hat. Not once in all the times he gave me these prickly offerings did it strike me that the day would come when I should find myself badly in need of a brace of hedgehogs.

By then, Danny was gone. I took Judy out on three nights running; just the kind of warm, balmy nights when I could hardly go a quarter of a mile in any direction with Danny and not hear him whining and yelping as he struggled to grasp the uncomfortable mouthful.

I led Judy to all the places where they were likely to be found, and I am certain we must have passed a dozen. If we did, she took no notice of them. She never does. I tried to do the job myself with a torch. No luck!

So Sally and Margie, who were camping on the lawn, slept undisturbed. Search as I would, I could not catch a couple of hedgehogs to put in their beds.

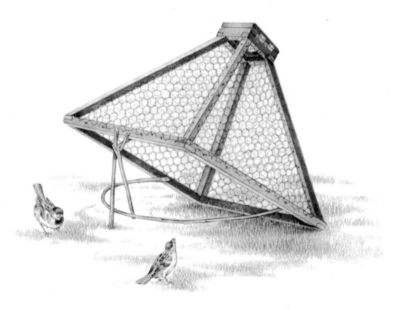

PART THREE

A Man at My Door

CHAPTER ELEVEN

COUNTRY FOLK

THERE was a cautious knock, and I opened the door to a fox of a gipsy whose leathery face was etched with seventy years of cunning.

Dog Judy, generally so welcoming to strangers, barked loudly as she sniffed at the threadbare trousers. Evidently she disapproved. But I have a feeling for the wandering craftsman who comes offering to ply his trade for an honest shilling. This one wanted dishes to mend.

The children went rooting in the rubbish heap and unearthed the two halves of a blue Spode dinner plate. We offered the gipsy a corner in our spacious kitchen, but he preferred to go to the bottom of the drive. Squatting by the road-side, a living advertisement for his own calling, he got busy. Sally and Margaret found sacks to sit on, and went to keep him company.

He was a character worth the meeting, with a tongue that could work as fast as his fingers. His implement, he said, was identical with drills used by the ancient Druids—a metal rod pointed with a tiny diamond (surely the Druids had no diamonds?) and weighted by a circular knob of stone. From the ends of a wooden cross-bar a leather thong went up and around the top of the rod. He moved the bar up and down; the thong made the drill revolve, and the stone fly-wheel kept it spinning. Deftly he pitted the broken plate with a double rank of hollows, and neatly he cut rivets of wire and cemented them in. When he had done the plate we gave him a vegetable dish, a jug, a soup tureen. We hunted out all the smashed china we could find.

From time to time Judy sneaked out and barked. She had not changed her mind, but neither had I. The whole scene charmed me. I was glad to have a gipsy with a Druid's drill working in the sunshine by the gateway of Wester Denhead. I was pleased to have my daughters sitting by him, listening to his talk of camp fires and roasted hedgehogs and life in a caravan. When no more bits and pieces could be discovered I was proud to call my wife and show her the array of mended crockery.

'All for a shilling or two,' I whispered, and asked the gipsy: 'How much?' Anxious to show that I was quite willing to pay for my pleasures, I added 'You must have been at it for a good three hours.'

'I charge sixpence a rivet,' he said pleasantly—and counted sixty-four!

We had a courteous discussion, the old fox and I, and our settlement for ten bob and a bundle of rabbit skins was made in so friendly a spirit that a month or two later he came back and paid me a high compliment. Not only did he remember my name, and those of the children, and even Judy's—the spaniel was voicing her protests the minute he appeared—but this time he was not seeking work. His call was for reasons of comradeship only.

He was in trouble. Not from any Tom, Dick or Harry would he deign to ask for help. He had travelled ten miles especially to see me.

'Ye ken what I am, sir—one o' the last o' the real old tinkers. I'm not a beggar.'

Someone had died, and there was to be a funeral in Aberdeen, and he was broke. Three pounds was the least that would do the job decently.

While I was counting out the notes, Judy was clearly saying 'No! No! No!' I rated her for her ill manners and chivvied her indoors. As security I accepted the diamond point of the Druid's drill, and for all I have ever heard since, the funeral might have been the gipsy's own. But the diamond is useful for cutting squares of glass to darken with candle-smoke whenever there is an eclipse of the sun!

The moral? None that I know of, unless that a man should listen to his hound instead of making up his own mind about foxy-faced customers who come telling hard-luck stories. Were I a townsman I could afford to have it engraved on brass and clamped to my gate 'No Hawkers. No Gipsies.' And underneath 'Beware of the Dog'.

But I am a countryman, and Judy's deep, instinctive distrust of the tinker tribe made no allowance for the chief thing that counted with me. They are vanishing. Their raggle-taggle encampments are being erased from woods and commons. Local authorities are inveigling them into houses, and their ragged broods into schools. Their sons are driving hydro-electric tunnels through the hills. Their daughters are dish-washing in great Highland hotels. And I am jealous of their going, because they are as much a part of the countryside I have loved as the forests that have been wiped out, the glens that have been flooded, the couthie home-made jollifications that have been ended by broadcasting dance-bands and buses to the cinema.

Not that I don't listen-in, and go to the movies. Not that I hold back my blessings from the makers of the artificial loch which lets me light my way to bed with the turn of a switch instead of stumbling upstairs shielding a candle-flame. Heavens, no! But still, it seems a pity. And so when the next one knocks and offers clothes-pegs or withy baskets, heather pot-scrubbers or besoms, he shall have my rabbit skins and my old boots and anything up to half the money he asks. He shall, too, have a welcome that will astonish him before it sets him scheming on how he can cash in.

The dish-mender was not the only one whom a friendly reception has brought back with a cunning story; not even the only one to choose death for his tale. But he was special. He had genius enough to clinch his argument with a piece of frank, shining truth.

'Ye ken what it's like, sir. There'll be relations from all over. Ach, at a time like that, ye have to stand your hand. . . .'

I have been at a tinker's funeral. I ken what it's like. I hope they had a hilarious time, and that no one came by the mishap which befell a pair at the one I attended. They tumbled into the grave, and a disgusted old crone, herself reeling dangerously on the brink, looked in at them sprawled on the coffin and began kicking at the clods of clay.

'Just beery the deevils!' she screamed.

Most of that company will have been buried by now, and their successors will do their best to forget that they have tinker blood, and that they have forfeited the kingdom of the countryside.

To whom? Among others, to neo-gipsies like myself who are glad to suffer the inconvenience of living four hundred miles from London, just for the delight of it.

Some of that delight is bound up with animals and birds, insects and fishes, and especially with dogs. It would be hard to imagine existence without them. But people matter more. Just as the tinkers must have their funerals and beanos, so we could not survive without, occasionally, a man at the door.

At least once every day, in the London boarding house where we first met, Mary and I used to hear our beloved Yorkshire landlady say:

'Eh, there's nowt so funny as folk!'

No one proved it more surely than Miss Roe herself. It is not only in the country places that 'characters' are met. She was a woman of courage, humour, and kindliness, and we like to think that whatever else of her faith she may have lost when one of the last of the flying bombs demolished the old house and buried her alive in the basement dining room, she still believed as they tried vainly to rescue her that nothing in the world makes so fascinating a show as the passing pageant of humanity.

A plague on those who say that men are becoming standardized! If a simple item like the human thumb is so distinct a thing that not two out of a hundred million carry the same markings, surely there can be individuality still in a complex affair like the human mind.

A word, then, about a few of the people who in one way or another have made life sweeter for us in this remoteness.

There was old Dr Grant. By his passing, our small community lost a personality. Myself, I liked him not only for his quiet, mellow mind, but also for the feeling he shared with me for a piece of good wood and the tools to shape it.

It was a pleasure merely to see him come out for his afternoon stroll in his dark, old-fashioned clothes. He was always spotless, his beard silvery and carefully trimmed, his well-carried figure and his lean, parchment face bearing a dignity and an elegance that belonged to a bygone day.

His death came about in a strange way. Walking one evening he came upon a small group of rifle-shooting enthusiasts, one of whom was consistently drilling pennies at twenty-five yards with the ·22.

The hole appeared so regularly in the dead centre of each penny that the doctor was very cool at first. He thought the shooters were playing a trick on him. But they convinced him at last, and asked:

Six weeks old

After the bath

Gippy

"Fetch your dish!"

Danny

Of them all, we have never kept a pleasanter one than Judy

141

'Like to have a go yourself, Doctor?'

He was game for anything. He loaded up, and as the penny was being placed for him there was the sound of a shot. The aged doctor did not so much fall as crumple up.

'I've shot myself,' he said.

Now it was the others who thought they were being tricked. But truly enough, in the rather shaky hands, the rifle had gone off accidentally.

His wound was only a minor one in the leg, but somehow it was enough to prick the frail casing of his vitality and let death come in. He lasted for only a few days.

As I have suggested, he never appeared in the streets but he was dressed with a careful, antique elegance. In his garden and workshop the clothes he wore were not only very old but very shabby.

He did not need to be parsimonious. It was only his little way, and he could be sensitive about being seen in this working garb. It seemed to hurt something in him to be caught out of uniform. Always, he liked to preserve that studied dignity, and yet he was not so small-minded a man that he did not have a sense of humour. He loved to tell against himself the story of the day when, in specially disreputable tatters, he was weeding his onion bed.

A seedy-looking character wandered into the garden, wheezed out a few notes from a mouth-organ, and extended a grubby hand. The doctor drew himself up, and I can imagine his stern and yet still kindly look.

'Why don't you find some work, instead of going about begging?' he said. 'There is plenty to do in a district like this—the potato fields, raspberry picking. Any farmer would give you a job if you asked for it.'

Under that sharp and knowing eye, no man could feel other than chastened.

'I—I've been thinkin' about tryin' . . .' Weary Willie muttered.

'You'll have to do more than think, man! Now tell me—what is your job when you do work?'

The tramp looked at the other ragged figure, and in comradeship edged closer.

'Just the same as yoursel',' he said. 'Odd jobs in gardens, an' the like o' that.'

The next one I shall call Janet, which might or might not have been her real name. There is no reason for taking trouble to hide her identity. Her family was not of the type to be ashamed of her being a washerwoman; they themselves possessed too many of her sterling qualities to be so foolish.

Janet was of the old-fashioned sort. She was a treasure. Those whom she served were well blessed, and most of them realized it and boasted about her.

Some friends of ours were suddenly struck with the thought that through the years when they had employed her on her humble task, Janet had done a lot of giving for which she had never taken. She had been paid for quantity, but never for quality. They thought it would be a pleasant thing to take her for a run in their car.

Janet was touched, and pleased. They picked her up, dressed in her best, and drove her through Dunkeld and up Tayside to Aberfeldy, along the shores of Loch Tay to Killin, and down to Lochearnhead.

At a beautiful spot on Loch Earn they opened a well-filled picnic basket, and in their company Janet enjoyed a delicious tea. Then home by way of Crieff and the Sma' Glen—as fine a run as even this glorious countryside can offer.

The sun shone all the way. The hills were purple; the water sparkled. The harvest stood in the fields. Flowers shone in cottage gardens. Janet, enchanted, sat up full of animation, looking to right and left, absorbing it all. Her keen interest was in itself a full reward for the trouble of giving her an afternoon's holiday.

Home again, she thanked our friends with a quiet grace and sincerity which moved them deeply.

'This has been a day I'll never forget,' she said, 'as long as I live.'

They asked her: 'What struck you most, of all you saw?'

She thought for a little time, as if sorting out the multitude of impressions which her busy eyes had given her.

'Well,' she answered, 'there was one thing. Maybe I shouldn't say it, but bein' Monday everybody's line was full —an' all the way, I never saw a whiter washin' than my own.'

I am in familiar company in the presence of a piece of wood and a few carpenter's tools, but metal and machines and even the simplest facts of mechanics are mysteries to me.

I tried, but failed, to work out the how and why of something which my old crony Sandy Ritchie told me he had once seen.

'It was just a little Shetland pony,' he told me, 'but it was ploughing a field of heavy clay all by itself—aye, and a double-furrow plough at that. A job that a pair of good young Clydesdales could never have managed.'

'How on earth . . .' I began.

'Pulleys,' said Sandy. 'The pony walked right round the field, you see, yoked to a long rope, and the plough crept up and down. Pulleys!'

I have no doubt Sandy was telling nothing but the plain truth. I simply don't understand pulleys, although I did, once, for an odd half-hour in my lifetime.

I walked into a school classroom on a visit to a section of an A T C unit and found the boys busy with a set of pulleys which they had fixed up with much string and ingenuity. On the one side hung a two-pound weight; on the other side, somehow balancing it, was a quarter-pound. When a penny was added to the quarter it sank slowly down, lifting the two pounds up.

'How does that come about?' I asked, and a budding airman told me, and for half an hour I knew. I understood. He made it all so crystal-clear that I even ventured to be bright on the subject of pulleys.

'A fine idea,' I said, 'to apply to a fishing rod. Instead of having to play a big fish for anything up to an hour, you could lift it right out . . .'

As I outlined my invention I noticed one youngster doing his best to hold himself together.

'What are you laughing at, Grant?' I demanded.

It took him a time to get breath, and then more time to be persuaded to share his joke, but at last he yielded it up

'Well, sir,' he exploded, 'what if it worked the wrong way round, and a wee fish pulled you in?'

To a writing man like myself, a visit to the local branch of the County Library means something more than the mere selection of a book or two for personal reading. I am a purveyor in the presence of possible customers. I am, as it were, on both sides of the counter at once, and therefore I keep my ears open and take note.

The comments which an author hears in such a place are, on the whole, saddening. Readers dither and swither among the thousands of volumes, grumbling because there is not a better selection. Almost the highest praise that one ever hears bestowed on a book is:

'That? Yes, it's not bad. Readable . . . in a way.'

I cherish only a single memory of a truly satisfied borrower. He is a farmer in a big way, and a good one. He has a genius for conjuring bountiful harvests out of the earth, and a rare eye for an animal. He is a man of real worth and quality.

He came striding into the library with a different look from the others. Plainly, he was a man who expected to get exactly what he wanted. He planked a volume on the desk.

'Gie's another book, lassie,' he said.

'What kind of one would you like this time?' the librarian asked him.

He neither swithered nor dithered. He knew.

'Ane wi' big print,' he said.

The librarian went to the shelves, thumbed through several, and picked one out.

'Will this do?'

He did not look at the title, nor at the author's name. He did not inquire whether it was thriller, straight novel or non-fiction. He opened it about the middle, looked at the type, and let out a grunt of deep approval.

'Perfect!' he said. 'Perfect!' And off he went.

If only I could cultivate the habit of keeping a diary, it would be full of incidents to disprove this dreary theory of standardization. The age of worthies is not past, and never will be.

It is true that Dr Grant, now, is a character out of yesterday, and that Sandy Ritchie could say, the last time I asked how he was keeping:

'Man, I'm spryer than ever! Once, I used to be that weak, if I came to a dike I'd loup it. Now—ach, I think nothing o' walkin' half a mile to find a gate!'

But the young ones are coming on. They have only to be given time.

At Wester Denhead we keep an ever-open door for all the children's friends. It is a perfect playground for youngsters, and not only Sally and Margie appreciate their company. In spite of their being educated, every one, in exactly the same way, it is still possible to tell t'other from which.

Little Helen is a classmate of Margie's, and she had no more than eight years on a day when I told her:

'You've been to a wedding.'

'What way d'ye ken?'

'I noticed a bit of confetti dropping out of your hankie.'

'My! You for a smartie! Aye, but I've been to a weddin' right enough. It was my auntie. Would you like me to tell you about it?'

Helen had missed nothing, especially about the bride's dress. She could say exactly how many tucks there were, and where; how the shoulders looked, and the sleeves. She could tell to a petal everything about the flowers in the bouquet, and when she had finished with the bride she started on the lady guests. I almost felt I had been at the wedding myself.

It was only the ladies she seemed to have noticed. For encouragement, I slipped in a question:

'How about the bridegroom?' I asked. 'You haven't told me what he was wearing. Don't say you didn't notice.'

'Oh—him!' Her lips curled in feminine contempt. Plainly Helen knew the exact value of a mere male at a wedding. 'Him! He was just in his workin' clothes.'

'His working clothes?' I said.

'Aye,' Helen shrugged. 'He's in the sodgers.'

CHAPTER TWELVE

INCOMPLETE ANGLER

ONLY fools so begrudge the passing years that they wish themselves back to infancy to begin all over again. Life is superlative fun, but if it is lived in the right way one round of the course should be enough. Childhood has a lot, but it misses a lot. One of the greatest things it misses is a full awareness of the delight of experiencing pleasant things for the first time. The first glimpse of the stars, the first flower, and bird song, and feel of the warmth of the sun—no one can remember them. If I were crazy enough to want to go back, it would be to pick up moments like those.

Having been all but born with a gun in my hands, I have no memory of when I first fired it, nor of what unholy joy I felt at my first shedding of blood. But it was different with fishing. That I took up only when I came back to the country, and so among my pleasures fishing stands unique.

Shooting seems so much part of the pattern of existence that I can do it as happily alone as in company. The comradeship of other guns is an added attraction, but not a necessity. The dog at heel is enough. It is different with fishing, which I have held over to this part of my book because it is concerned not so much with fish as with other men.

Chief among these was the doctor. I always knew why, in the shooting field, I saw and therefore killed more game than he did. That was simply because he had no dog. But when the guns were laid by and the rods taken out, there was a mysterious change in the order of things. He never failed to give me my choice of ends of the boat or reaches of the river—and whichever end or reach I picked, the fish were always at his. We would change over, and they followed him.

Since he went away nearly two years ago not a line have I dipped. My box of dry flies, with its quaint sections each fitted with a glazed lid which springs open at a touch, is Margie's plaything. My casts are rotting for want of use. It was the doctor at my door who used to get me into thigh-boots and away, and I miss the delightful hours we spent together at the water.

It cost him an effort to get the fever started. He was going to Caithness on holiday, to the gracious old house where his doctor-wife's doctor-father lived in retirement. For weeks he talked about the lochs in those parts; about the sporting trout of Watten; the great, plump fish of Heilen; the countless ones of Calam, so eager for the fly that once I got among them I should catch them by the score, and so ever after be another disciple of ancient Isaac.

'Come,' he said, 'and spend the last week with us.'

His fishy tales, had he known it, cut no more ice than had his advice that if I halved my smoking I might be less breathless when going uphill. I went, but only for the enjoyment of good company.

Having, in the last chapter, tried to raise a smile or two at the expense of some acquaintances, it might only be fair to offer one against myself.

Either by road or rail Caithness seems very remote. The easiest way to get there was by air, and in those days a passenger service operated from Perth. So, on a fine morning, to the aerodrome at Scone, complete with rod and modest suit-case, to be weighed and assigned a seat.

In build I am something of a Cassius, with a lean and hungry look. Where, as in air travel, weight is a matter of importance, the advantage is always with the airline when it carries men like me.

'No reduction for skeletons?' I asked in my best Aberdeen accent.

'No reduction!'

My luggage, too, was put on the scales. I had taken the barest minimum, a mere handful, but even at that it was found to be the odd pound or two beyond the permitted free limit.

'There's an excess charge,' I was told, 'of ninepence.'

What could Aberdeen do but grumble?

'It's those fishing boots, sir,' the courteous official explained. 'They're heavy, you know.'

So I sat down on a nearby chair, and proceeded to unfasten my shoelaces.

'I'm changing into the boots,' said I, 'and then they'll be part of my own weight. Fair enough?'

I saved my ninepence—and travelled in shoes.

Besides being the first fishing expedition, this was the first flight—up through the clouds and over the Grampians, whose peaks were thrusting above the surface of a sun-splashed sea of cotton wool.

At Wick there were no clouds. May was never more fragrantly warm. It was a day to make a traveller greet his hosts with laughter and bursting gratitude. But the doctor, most equable of men, was scarcely so much as smiling. When I began to praise the quality of the weather he had laid on, I soon sensed that I had dropped a brick.

'This ghastly sunshine!' he said. 'Day after day!'

'Ghastly?'

'It's the worst May on record!'

'It's been continuously sunny at home,' I said. 'We can't get the children to wear more than bathing costumes. Not a breath of wind . . .'

'Just the same here. Not a breath. Let's hope you've brought a change. I've caught less than a dozen all week.'

There was no change. Each morning dawned brighter than the last. Forenoon and afternoon we rowed on unruffled water, casting and casting again. About twice a day the doctor's line whirred; mine not at all, and I dared not tell him how little I cared. Never having caught a fish in my life, I did not feel I was missing anything.

The last day arrived. We got up early, but not so early as the sun. The tips of the tall trees around Old Hall, in which numberless rooks had their nests, showed not a shiver of motion.

'You'll catch a fish today,' the doctor promised, 'whatever the weather does.'

We set off across miles of moorland towards the loch where, let the sun do its damnedest and the wind sulk all day, the trout never failed to oblige. At the appointed place we met Uncle Jack, whose sheep grazed the moors. This tanned and sunny-hearted gentleman, one of the keenest and best anglers in Caithness, had allied himself with the doctor in a single, unbending purpose. I was not to be allowed to touch an oar. I was not to waste time fumbling over changes of flies. Despite his seventy years and the many calls of a busy life, he was to be gillie for the day. I was merely there to catch a fish.

Nothing but this fish was talked about as we drove to the end of the track and finished the journey on foot. I dared not mention the wonderful blue of the water when at last we came upon it; the gold of the stretch of sand by the boathouse; the thrill of finding anything so beautiful, so far from anywhere. A hen grouse fluttered up from our feet and landed on the opposite side of a burn. Not a word could I let myself say about her brood of chicks, isolated on the wrong bank. They plopped into the water and swam across as confidently as ducklings.

We got out the boat, and we fished. For two hours we worked, flogging the water. Never a rise. Never a ring anywhere on the glassy surface.

This constant working of the rod was growing very tiresome to an unaccus-tomed wrist.

'It doesn't seem to be of much use . . .' I began.

'Keep on fishing!'

Another hour, and suddenly, with as much excitement as if the heavens had burst open and Gabriel himself had appeared, there was a shout:

'You have a fish on!'

I looked at the doctor's rod. It was uncurved, the line slack.

'You! You!'

I gave a startled jerk—and away went my line, the reel singing, and up my arm and through the whole of this mortal frame there shivered for the first time that strange, electric thrill of feeling a struggling fish at the far end of a stick and a bit of string. It was, and always will be, a rare and rousing sensation. It does not have the sudden finality of shooting down a bird. It is prolonged, so that a man can savour it. It is—and I wish I had thought of telling Jack Davidson as much—a greater, a sharper, a more satisfying thrill than one can ever get with a gun.

The trout leapt out of the water, and instantly they knew, both Uncle Jack and the doctor, that its weight was around the eight-ounce mark. They could not have been more excited or more urgently helpful if it had been a sixty-pound salmon.

'Don't touch the reel!' 'Reel in now!' 'Drop your rod point!' 'Hold your rod up!' 'Bring it in!' 'Let it run!'

The accommodating fish which had hooked itself as I gazed at the golden sand had done a thorough job. It stayed on through all my fumblings. After ten minutes of tortured ecstasy, there was Uncle Jack making a swipe with an outsize landing-net. My fish was in the boat.

Every tug of it is remembered; every sound of the reel; every agony as the line slackened; every heart-beat of relief as contact was felt again. But in the memory, there is one thing still sharper.

It was as I posed in the stern of the boat, catch in hand, to be photographed by Dr Jean, while Dr Alastair and Uncle Jack looked on. Uncle Jack gave a sigh, a deep, long sigh of something more than satisfaction, more than wonder.

In it, so it seemed to me, there were recollections of legions of trout and salmon which he himself had caught in all kinds of circumstances over the long years; of ones that got away and ones that were defeated by a thousand crafty moves.

Uncle Jack's mind was rich; rich with fishing experiences which could be taken out and lived over again. But just then, in one way, as an angler I was richer than he.

Gazing at me, that great old sportsman had something of the look of a husband just admitted to the bedside of his wife and his firstborn, and the thing I recall with most emotion is him turning to the doctor and saying, in a whisper of genuine awe:

'His *first* fish!'

Thus did I catch a trout—although it might be more true to say that in more ways than one the trout had caught me. When we got back, the doctor had no difficulty in persuading me to apply for membership of the Blairgowrie Angling Club, just in time to take part in one of the club's outings to Loch Leven.

This fantastic loch is known to fishing men the world over. Stock from it has been taken to waters as far afield as New Zealand. Each year it yields up something like sixty thousand trout, the average weight being just under a pound.

In angling, there are no class distinctions. On the pier at Loch Leven I have seen coal-miners swapping yarns with colonels, labourers with lords. But in the company of the expert fishers of Blairgowrie I felt very small beer as I followed the doctor into one of the big, heavy boats which require two oarsmen, and sat down in the stern facing old Sandy.

'Where would you like to go, sir?'

Well did I know that this veteran, who must have seen tons of fish caught, was bound to discover that one of his passengers was a greenhorn.

'So far as I'm concerned,' said I, 'it makes very little difference. I've caught only one trout in my lifetime, and that took me the whole of last week. It'll be nothing short of miraculous if I get another one tonight.'

The murmur of the water, the slaps of leaping fish

This was not meant as any sort of challenge, but only an expression of proper humility. It seemed to pierce Sandy to the quick. It inspired him. He looked at all the other boatloads of competitors making off in the direction of the famous island where Mary Queen of Scots was once imprisoned; weighed the situation shrewdly; looked at the sky, tested the wind, and scanned the whole area of the loch.

'We'll try the south shore,' he said.

One other boat followed us. Otherwise, overwhelmingly, the majority opinion was against Sandy. It did not seem to matter. As we glided towards the small wood which fringes a part of the south shore, I pulled out thirty yards of line and trolled, while Sandy talked.

He talked about fish and fishermen; but especially, and with biting scorn, about the kind of fishermen who come to Loch Leven and take note of the phenomenon which royal Mary, from her prison window, may well have seen with pleasure.

'Sunsets!' said Sandy, and spat into the water. 'They rave about the sunsets! Ma Goad. . . .'

Even as he spoke, the tumbled clouds were gathering a varied majesty of shimmering tints. The bouncing waves were flecked with gold and crimson, and the beauty of the scene was something to remember. Having been warned, I held my tongue. Even when I looked I looked secretly, pretending to be busy with the trailing line.

'Man, you've got a fish on!'

That was number two, which Sandy saw before I felt it—and, as I played it, what a fish! A veritable monster of the loch! Even old Sandy, so he declared, had seldom seen one run so far and so fast; one which struggled so stubbornly and so strongly. The aged boatman was positive that his tyro passenger had hooked one which was destined to end its days proudly displayed in an outsize glass case, and he was desperate to see it safely in the boat.

Not a finger did he put on my rod, for this was a competition. Nevertheless, it was he and not I who captured that fish, each of us all but tumbling out of the boat in excitement as he gasped out advice.

It was conquered at last, and netted. One pound; none of us could make it more. There was a simple reason for its having put up so powerful a battle —and not my want of skill, either.

My second trout was caught by the tail.

Whenever an angler begins to share his simple reminiscences, suspicion always rears its ugly head. Being a fisherman is like being an Aberdonian—the constant butt of the same old joke. As for being an Aberdonian fisherman, it is almost too much to bear.

What use to vow that in this part of this book, as all the way through it, I am not setting down a word which is not the plain truth? What sense in finishing my account of that evening on Loch Leven without offering some proof that it is not mere romancing?

The Blairgowrie Angling Club, I hope, keeps records; and among them, I trust, is one obscure line to bear me out.

That evening, listening to Sandy's unceasing stream of advice, I took nine fine trout; the doctor, going his own way, had a tidy dozen. As we rowed back on the edge of midnight I watched the other boats, bearing all the best fishers from Blairgowrie, as they emerged from the darkness. I expected to see them almost swamped with fish.

The first we hailed was the only other which had gone with us to the south shore. The two men in it had thirty fish between them. On the pier, clutching my modest basket, I spoke to the others as they came to land.

'Any luck?' 'How were things?'

Nothing but long faces! Nothing but groans! Two here; a singleton there; many a basket empty.

We went to the scales. We weighed up. The doctor took third prize and I took the fourth, and I've been crowing about it ever since!

Once upon a time (and there could be no more fitting opening for this episode) the local A T C squadron went camping at R A F, Montrose. Before we set out, a kindly friend offered two shrewd tips to myself and my fellow-officers.

'Take your rods,' he said. 'And when you pay your courtesy call on the Group Captain, mention that you're keen on fishing.'

This Jeff and Mervyn and I did, and so came by way of an experience which, but for having each other to verify it, we could separately hardly believe.

The Group Captain needed but the word, the merest hint. Already our cadets had been received with the most astonishing hospitality, and now it was our turn. The subject of angling had scarcely been more than touched when Groupie was telephoning to Flight-Lieutenant Smith.

'There are three A T C officers . . . they fish . . . will you see what you can do . . .?'

We trekked to the office of Flight-Lieutenant Smith, and there we learned that the owner of Aldbar Castle, near Brechin, had put his home and everything within it at the disposal of the officers' mess of R A F, Montrose; a gesture which gained him a deal more gratitude than he can ever have heard of, however often he was thanked.

With the castle went the freedom of something like three miles of the South Esk, the fabled, carefully preserved South Esk; *carte blanche* to three miles of it, and all that therein swam.

Even before the ice had broken and we had discovered him as a fellow-spirit, Smith struck us as a man of quality, competence to his finger-tips. He gave us chairs around his desk and, pulling out a clean sheet of foolscap, he proceeded to pass out the 'gen'. Across the length of the paper he drew two wiggly and roughly parallel lines.

'This is the end of the beat. Now here, at this bend, is the first pool. Lying in it there is a shoal of just over two hundred sea trout. We come along here, to this stretch. Close under the far bank there you'll find a small shoal; perhaps thirty. Now the second big pool, here. There are three hundred fish in that. They can be reached from either side. Then you'll find perhaps a dozen here . . .'

Whether or not they shared my amazed incredulity as the tale went on, Jeff and Mervyn had the courtesy to keep silent. Not I, who never possessed the golden gift. When we came to the last pool in the magical stretch, and its fishy inhabitants had been counted to the last head, I had to say:

'D'you know their Christian names, too?'

'Don't you believe me?'

The retort was uncomfortably direct. I squirmed a little.

'I'll show you. It'll only take fifteen minutes,' said Flight-Lieutenant Smith.

He packed us into a plane, and off we went to Aldbar. From five thousand feet we saw the stretch of water, just as it had been on paper; the weir, the different pools, the groups of trees, everything.

'Now we'll go down and see the fish.'

We went down, three rather jittery flyers in the hands of a superbly experienced pilot. We tilted sideways, and while our hearts were still in our mouths the Flight-Lieutenant pointed to a piece of water which was fairly leaping up to meet us.

'About a couple of hundred, wouldn't you say?'

And there they were; just, I should say, about a couple of hundred sea-trout, and so clearly visible that it was quite easy to assess their various sizes and actually to see the wiggles of their tails.

'Now the next stretch . . .'

There was no need to go on, but we went on. Smith's was no angler's yarn. We were prepared to swear that not in one of the pools had he exaggerated by so much as a single fish.

We flew back to Montrose, and as we stepped dizzily to earth again, a smile which was not nearly so much triumphant as comradely flashed across the face of Flight-Lieutenant Smith.

'Hope you have luck,' he said, 'tomorrow night.'

We were to start fishing with the dusk, and carry on through the small hours. But first we were to dine in Aldbar Castle, and after our arms had tired of pulling out the sea-trout, we were to pass the remainder of the night housed within its venerable walls.

Those readers who have castles of their own may well skip the rest of this chapter; unless, indeed, they be like Jack Davidson, and have a feeling for someone who does a good thing for the first time.

It was not that I had not, on occasions, dined in quite select places. Nor was this the first castle I had entered. But it was certainly the first I had owned. Each of us separately, Jeff and Mervyn and I, had that feeling. The castle was ours.

Not only so, but besides the competent housekeeper who was busying herself over our comfort, we had three lackeys to wait upon us hand and foot. Our friend Flight-Lieutenant Smith was there, with no other wish but to translate into reality our dreams of taking baskets of those sea-trout. With him was Flying Officer Stirling, all the way from Australia, who not so long before had had the experience of nose-diving from five thousand feet, and unable to burst open the escape-door from the plane. It crashed, and he discovered himself walking round the matchwood wreckage, not so very much the worse.

The third lackey was Squadron Leader Betty, Commandant of our camp, a regular R.A.F. officer whom I have good reason to remember with gratitude and regard.

On the evening of a perfect day, Jeff and Mervyn and I strolled round the policies of our domain, inspecting our woods, our gardens, our cottages. We walked up the winding stairs and through the corridors of our castle, looking at our fine furniture, our paintings and *objets d'art*, our library with its shelves of beautifully bound books.

Under soft lights in our panelled dining-room we dined, and then, leisurely to the river.

The sea-trout had not departed. The water was boiling with them. We put up our rods and began to fish, while our faithful attendants, their pockets well filled with refreshments, liquid and solid, kept plying us with snacks.

The very night itself seemed to have taken on something of the quality of unreality which pervaded the whole scene. It was still and warm and clear; almost the only sounds the murmur of the water, the slaps of leaping fish, and the swish of our lines.

A perfect night. Perfect, and incredible, and it is pleasant to think how many flying men, who deserved it and needed it so much more than I, enjoyed the same fairy-tale ownership of Aldbar Castle.

We fished, and we fished, and when the first signs of dawn began to appear we went home to our venerable abode, while the sea-trout still splashed and slapped restlessly in the low, clear pools, waiting impatiently for the spate that would enliven them and send them racing up to the spawning beds.

The catch? Just two, and neither to my rod; two, and both accidentally foul-hooked, for on such a night fish are not to be taken.

Betty, and Smith, and Stirling, and later the Group Captain himself, were mortified at our 'disappointment'. Doubtless the owner of Aldbar Castle would have been so too, had he known of it. Our friends at R A F, Montrose, urged us to go back and try again, and it may be that they did not understand why we three refused.

It was only because we felt that even a record catch could add nothing to perfection; and a second visit might prove that after all we had not stepped out of pure reality into something so rare and fragile that to keep it whole it must never be touched again.

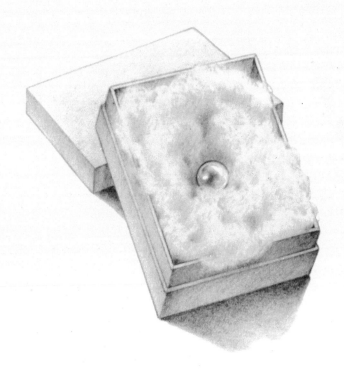

CHAPTER THIRTEEN

ON THE WAY

LIVING as we do in the service of so many birds, animals, and insects, we find it a major operation to get away from them all for more than a few hours at a time. But a housewife must escape from housework now and again, and a writing man must occasionally look beyond his own door for human contacts.

It was my English wife who first pointed out to me the difference between travelling in her countryside and mine. When we took train from Paddington to her home in the west, we would sit talking in hushed voices to one another while the rest of the compartment read its paper or ate its sandwiches or conversed in the same discreet whispering. When we set off from King's Cross for Scotland, we knew all our fellow-travellers before we were out of the station. We chattered all the way among a company of friends.

Nothing annoys me more than the brother Scot who with a few scoffing words wipes the English off the map as an inferior race. This observation of the contrast between a journey from Paddington and one from King's Cross is not meant to prove anything of the kind. But I do think that those English people, and others, who keep themselves to themselves in the presence of strangers are missing a lot.

Wherever I go, I must talk to whomsoever I meet. My wife has grown used to it. I think she even enjoys it. Casual meetings are full of charm—and sometimes surprises.

We were in a train once heading for Aberdeen, and opposite us, the only two other occupants of the compartment, were a couple of men.

They were an oddly assorted pair; the one soberly but smartly dressed in blue suit, dark coat, and soft hat, the other shoddy-looking, frayed about the trousers, and wearing a greasy cap.

Although there were two empty corners they sat close together, and yet they seemed to have very little to say to one another. The one in the hat was a taciturn fellow, but his companion's eyes brightened the minute I spoke to him. He was ready and willing to talk.

His subject was pearls. His profession was fishing for them—not in the oyster-beds in any remote Pacific seas, but right there in Aberdeenshire, in the River Ugie.

The unostentatious Ugie flows very near my birthplace, but I had never known that its water concealed anything so romantic as pearls.

'They're got out of the fresh-water mussels,' our new acquaintance said, and looked to his friend for confirmation. The other grunted his assent in a way which shut out all doubt.

We heard how the water was searched by laying a glass-bottomed box on the surface; how the mussels were fished up, and opened and examined.

'And are they like real pearls?' Mary asked.

'But they are real pearls, Mum. Of course, a lot of them are black or brown or mottled, but now and then you get a right one—a real beauty.' He added, smiling his pleasure at our interest: 'I've one in my pocket now. A topper!'

We asked if we might see it. Again he glanced at the other man, who once again grunted. Our friend brought from the pocket of his ragged jacket a small, oblong box. He did not use both hands to open it. He lifted the lid awkwardly with his teeth and then, fixing it between his knees, he removed a wad of cotton wool.

There, truly enough, nestling on more cotton wool, was a pearl; a beautiful,

11

softly coloured, perfectly formed pearl, still innocent of string or gold mount. We rolled it in our palms. We exclaimed over it, and especially over the miracle of its having been found in that river of all places.

'Which stretch of the Ugie did it come from?' I asked.

He gave a laugh.

'When ye ken a thing like that, ye keep it to yoursel'.'

But I had hardly murmured my apologies for putting an improper question when he was giving me the full story. He spared no trouble in fixing the exact spot; the nearby cottage, the twisted tree, the boulder on the bank. In detail he described again the whole method of getting the mussels, but still more than that.

'If ye want to have a try,' he said, 'I'll tell ye where my house is. Go, an' say I sent ye. Ye'll get a lend o' the kit . . .'

The other man jogged his elbow. He stopped. The train was just running into the station at Aberdeen, and as the two rose to go we noticed for the first time that they were handcuffed together.

In another chapter I have written with some warmth of the beauties of parts of Germany. We saw and liked these before we discovered that Scotland itself holds scenes as fair as anything in the Rhineland, the Black Forest, or Bavaria.

As for the charm of meeting people of a different race—Scotland can offer that too. I am a Lowlander, with no attachment to any clan, and so my children can range through the whole book of designs when they are picking a tartan for their next kilt. The Gaelic-speaking Highlander is another kind of man, and an excursion into his country is as rewarding as any trip abroad.

A run down the Caledonian Canal in May, with the birches springing into leaf, is as good a run as anyone could wish for—whether or not the Loch Ness Monster presents himself as an added attraction.

We saw him. We pulled up and watched him for quite a time. We had an excellent view of him in clear sunlight, and although it may seem the grossest disloyalty to a district which we like passionately, nothing now will ever convince us that he is composed of anything more substantial than water, riffled into long, sportive waves by a south-west wind.

It was in this incomparable countryside that we noticed a mountain with a quaint shape. The dark of its shadowy side splotched with patches of late snow, it looked astonishingly like a gargantuan spaniel resting alertly among the surrounding hills.

It did not matter much that when the snow had melted the illusion would be gone—it was as good an excuse as any other to stop and meet some of the natives.

At a very tidy little wayside railway station an aged porter was dutch-hoeing imaginary weeds from an immaculate platform. We called his attention to Spaniel Hill, and asked him what was its real name.

He had no idea. He was a stranger in those parts. But as we have proved a hundred other times, the Highlander is a true gentleman. He, too, likes meeting other folk. He took us to the station master; introduced us as if we were friends, and passed on our inquiry about the hill.

The station master was delighted to have this oddity of his own landscape pointed out to him. He declared that he saw the likeness to a dog at once—but he could not give the dog a name.

'We'll find out, though,' he said. 'Hamish will know.'

'Hamish?' There seemed to be only the two men in that part of the world.

'Up at the signal cabin. It's not far.'

He escorted us along the lineside to the tall signal cabin, and called out something in Gaelic. A window slid open, and there was Hamish; a round-faced, smiling, pleasant fellow with the same liquid music in his voice as the other two.

'That hill?' said Hamish. 'It's called Màm Bàn.'

'Can you tell us,' I asked, 'what that means in English?'

He did not answer at once. He wrinkled his brows, giving the question due consideration.

'Well . . . màm, that's a kind of a humph, you see, and bàn—what would I say? Fair, now, or maybe pale, or white. It would mean the fair hill, or the white hill.'

But apart from the patches of snow it looked to our eyes almost a black hill; and if it were sometimes entirely snow-covered, so would all its neighbours be. The station master and the signalman discussed all this gravely, breaking into the Gaelic now and then, but always careful to give a translation of what they were saying.

'Have you the dictionary, Hamish?' the station master asked at last.

The signal cabin of a remote Highland station seemed an unlikely place to look for a dictionary. But Hamish nodded, and the volume which he brought and laid open on the window ledge high above our heads was no vest-pocket affair but a big, leather-bound tome; the lexicon of a man of erudition. Hamish turned its pages with the smooth, confident movements of a man who knew his way among books, of a student performing a pleasant and familiar task.

He found his definitions and read them out to us from his elevated pulpit. This word, 'màm', was indeed 'a kind of humph'—a round, slowly rising hill; a swelling or boil; or also, if you wished, a double handful of any granulated substance. Hamish discoursed upon the various meanings, and upon words in general, their origins, the links between one language and another, and the first beginnings of human speech as it developed out of incoherent sounds and signs.

Màm Bàn meant exactly what he had said it meant, and the signalman was at pains to assure us that although the hill looked dark just then, there was much limestone in its geological composition, and when the sun was shining the other way it looked pale or white or fair.

Not until a bell began to tinkle did we tear ourselves away and travel on, enriched, leaving Hamish to his studies and his duties.

A mile or two farther and we came upon an old, old man standing lonely by a cottage gate. He was erect and proud of carriage, a figure of dignity and wisdom, and merely for the pleasure of meeting him we stopped and asked him the name of the hill which looked like a resting spaniel.

'Achmawhoople,' he said. Or so it sounded.

'Can you spell it for me?'

'Easily! A-C-H-P-H-U-B-L-E.'

It happened to be one of the times when the tobacco tax had just taken another leap. This oldster was sucking an empty pipe, and there was a sorrow in his eye. The best I could offer was a cigarette. With an apology he broke it up, and thrust it into the well-seasoned bowl, and set it going.

'Are you sure the hill is Ach . . . whatever you said?' I asked. 'It isn't Màm Bàn?'

He had never heard of Màm Bàn, but he was still sure. He had been born just on the other side of it, in a lonely shepherd's cottage miles from any other habitation. He rolled back the years for us and took us with him into his boy-hood: trudging to church of a Sunday, herding, listening to the whir of his grandmother's spinning-wheel. He told us, in the course of an hour's chat about olden times, the circumstances of his grandfather's death at the Battle of Waterloo.

We enjoyed the old veteran, and we enjoyed Hamish. Either, alone, would have made that day worth living for us. When we reached Fort William we bought a one-inch Ordnance Survey map of their district, not with any desire to prove one of them wrong, but only to look at the contours of the hill which their talk had made into something more than a lump of earth and rock, and more than a nature-sculptured spaniel.

We searched diligently, but although that peak was certainly of an eminence to get itself mentioned on the map, we could find neither Màm Bàn nor Ach-phuble.

I feel compelled to put one more experience on record.

The train, on this occasion, was bound for Inverness. The man opposite me, whose name I never knew, had the look of one who had done a deal of travelling. His keen, intelligent face had the tan of foreign suns.

Somewhere on the early stages of the journey we passed within sight of a shapely white ferro-concrete bridge, modern as the day's paper, spanning a roistering burn as old as the world's oldest hills. Near it, abandoned but remaining, was the hump-backed relic it had replaced.

The stranger remarked that the new bridge was a fine piece of work. I countered by saying that I liked the old one better.

'I have a fondness,' I said, 'for ancient stones.'

He looked at me in a quizzical way, fished in his waistcoat pocket with finger and thumb, and brought out a small object.

'D'you know what that is?'

My own finger and thumb went to my own pocket, and I laid my exhibit on my palm next to his. It is quite conceivable that we were the only two men in Britain that day going about our affairs each with a flint arrowhead in his possession, and there we were sitting opposite each other in an Inverness train.

He told me about his, and it was an interesting story. He had picked it up in Canada when he was supervising the construction of a new bridge. The excavators had dug into an historic burial ground of the Red Indians, and in deference to the feelings of their present-day successors an alteration had been made in the plans. His arrowhead was a souvenir.

I told him about mine and the many more I had at home, picked up in East Aberdeenshire by my father and his brothers as they worked the land.

Soon my friend was asking:

'Have you heard about the five stones in the churchyard at Rothiemurchus?'

'I've never even heard about Rothiemurchus.'

'A beautiful spot. Just at the foot of the Cairngorms. You get off at Avie-more, and it's about a mile. Wonderful scenery—pines, hills, burns, glorious walks. These five stones are on the grave of Farquhar Shaw. He had a Gaelic name, but I can't pronounce it. He was the survivor of the famous battle on the North Inch at Perth—when? Oh, centuries ago. Twenty-five men of his clan had a fight to the death with twenty-five from Clan Chattan . . .'

For a time we were diverted to history, but we soon got back to the subject of ancient stones, and in particular to the five on the grave of Farquhar Shaw at Rothiemurchus.

They were, he said, cylindrical blocks of granite, about the size of farmhouse cheeses, and they rested on the grass above the six-centuries-old tomb.

'Are you superstitious?' he asked.

'Not so much as one per cent.'

'Neither am I, and yet . . . well, it's odd. The stones are loose, you know, not fixed to anything. They're quite easily picked up. But it's said—I'm only saying it's said, and I don't really believe it—that anyone who disturbs them falls under a curse. Something terrible happens. You know the sort of idea. The funny thing is that I know a fellow who tipped them over, just for the devil of it, and it's perfectly true that only the next day, when he was climbing, he had a serious fall and broke both his legs.'

An individual who had until then been buried behind a newspaper put it down and joined the discussion.

'He was lucky,' he said.

'Lucky?'

This other fellow-traveller, quoting names and dates, mentioned a chauffeur who had also flung the five stones off Farquhar Shaw's grave. Within a week he was killed in a car smash.

'Coincidence!' I said.

'You can't believe in that much coincidence.'

'I can believe in any amount of it. Look at us two, both carrying flint arrowheads.'

The trip passed very pleasantly. I was on my way to Inverness to fix up accommodation for a prolonged working holiday. This part of my native land was then strange to me, and as the train drew towards Aviemore Junction both men began pointing out the beauties of the Cairngorms, and the Spey, and the lochs and the woods. The decision came to me impulsively.

'I'm getting off here,' I said.

'I thought you were going all the way . . .'

'Must settle an argument with those five stones in the churchyard at Rothie-murchus!'

THE GRAVE OF
SEATH MÓR SGORFHIAGLACH
VICTOR IN THE COMBAT
AT PERTH IN 1396

Anyone who disturbs them falls under a curse

That last remark was nothing but a piece of fun. It was my first glimpse of the Cairngorms which had captivated me. I hired a cycle and went scouting around, and the more I saw the more I was certain that here more than anywhere else could my family enjoy a change of air. I booked at an hotel and went home without troubling to go near any churchyard.

At the same time, those stones were not forgotten. They seemed to offer a kind of challenge.

We arrived at Aviemore in early April, long before the first of the tourists had put in an appearance, and stayed until the end of May. In that quiet off-season there were never more than a dozen people in the hotel at one time, and that was a priceless advantage. We got to know each other. We were like a family, and ourselves by far the least interesting of a fascinating company.

In the next chapter I want to tell something of them, and especially of two of them. But first—about the grave of Farquhar Shaw.

It is said that the man who boldly and ostentatiously walks under a ladder is proving himself just as superstitious as the man who goes carefully round it. It may be so—but what else is one to do except bump into it? With my wife I cycled to see the churchyard at Rothiemurchus, and found it on the whole a depressing place in the midst of so much beautiful scenery. The tiny old church had its windows boarded up. The atmosphere seemed gloomy and somehow desolate and deserted.

The grave of Farquhar Shaw was easily found. Its original headstone has sunk into the ground so that only a few inches are left showing. Clamped to it is a crude, cast-iron plate which claims that the man it commemorates was the victor in the combat.

In the meantime I had been reading some of the history of the battle, but I must have read the wrong book, or not taken it in aright. The information I had gleaned was that five of Chattan's men, although all wounded, were left alive and in possession of the field, while the single survivor on the other side only just managed to save his bacon by jumping into the Tay and swimming to safety. It matters very little. He has been a long time dead, either way.

I picked up one of the five granite blocks.

'Put it down!' said my wife.

'I'm going to fling them off. All five of them.'

'No! Please don't do it! No!'

Mary is not superstitious either, but:

'You never know,' she said.

I was not very specially anxious to move them, although I had meant to do it. As it was, I contented myself by making some impudent remarks about men whose tombstones told lies. I put the block back, and went wandering looking for birds' nests as Mary made a sketch.

For no reason to which I would care to give a name, I feel I must mention that three evenings later, when we were sitting in the lounge after dinner, the telephone bell rang. I looked up at my wife with a grin.

'Isn't it marvellous,' I said, 'to hear that and know it's not for me?'

The telephone is the bane and plague of my life, and practically no one knew where we were. But presently the manageress appeared.

'The call is for you . . .'

It was to summon me to the deathbed of one of my nearest and dearest relations.

Not for anything will I ever believe that this had the remotest connection with five lumps of granite on the grave of Farquhar Shaw in the churchyard at Rothiemurchus, Inverness-shire.

CHAPTER FOURTEEN

TO THE HILLS

THE view to the eastward from the birch-clad slopes behind Aviemore is one of the finest and fairest in Britain. Beyond the swift-running Spey stretches what remains of the ancient Forest of Rothiemurchus, and farther, but still intimately near, is the compact group of the Cairngorms.

These are friendly, approachable hills. Sturdy children may walk to the top of Cairngorm itself, or reach the high summit of Ben Muich Dhui or the great plateau of Braeriach where, mysteriously, the springs which are the source of the Royal Dee gush out at a place which is within a hundred or two feet of being the highest land in this country.

Cutting between the high tops is the Lairig Ghru pass, by which a hardy

171

walker may make his way to the beauties of Deeside, meeting as he goes the red deer, the ptarmigan, and the golden eagle itself.

We set out for Aviemore equipped with stout shoes and still stouter resolutions. We were to conquer those Cairngorms, every one of them. We had no ice-axes, alpenstocks, or ropes. The routes which we had planned for ourselves avoided carefully the rocky ascents which are the delight of the true mountaineers. All sorts, from novices to experts, may enjoy themselves in this enchanted country. Our ambitions were modest, but nevertheless high.

We had scarcely arrived when we were scrambling up the thousand feet of Craigellachie, conveniently placed for practice just behind the hotel, and although we soon felt puffed and stiff about the thighs, the triumph of that small conquest was an enticement and a spur.

As it turned out, we did not attempt a single Cairngorm. The weather was good. Others set off, and came back with glowing tales of the view, the exhilaration, the spiritual uplift. For us the summits remain a pleasure awaiting another day.

A few turns up some of the nearby slopes, and we had both the wind and the energy for the job. It was not that. We were simply so busy doing other things that we never got round to mountaineering. Although we had taken neither rod nor gun, we spent most of the time hunting.

A few days after our arrival there stepped off the evening train and walked briskly into the hotel a Captain of the Royal Navy. He dined briefly, and we were still lingering over coffee when he reappeared, passing the window, dressed in comfortable old tweeds and carrying a long-handled net.

Dusk was already gathering. He was back within half an hour, and as I manœuvred my family flotilla to make room for him by the lounge fire I asked him:

'Were you having a trial cast? Anything rising?'

'I don't fish,' he said.

'I thought I saw you going out with a landing net . . .'

He looked at me with the direct and disconcerting gaze of a man of the sea. 'That was a butterfly net.'

For a moment it seemed to me that I had talked out of turn, and that the answer was no more than an invitation to mind my own business. I grunted and picked up a book. But the children took up where I had left off.

'Did you catch any butterflies?'

'One moth.'

'What kind?'

Sally turned her blind eye to my signals for silence.

'Kentish Glory,' said the Captain.

'Male or female?'

'It's a lady.'

In my ear, but loud enough for the Captain to hear, a whisper:

'Oh, Daddy, I wish I could see it!'

The Captain left the room, and I was still lecturing my family on the sin of talking too much when he reappeared carrying what looked like an extra large pill-box with a glass bottom.

'There it is!'

We were not entirely strangers to the beauties and wonders of the moth world. The previous year we had collected a couple of dozen furry caterpillars, and had seen them go into cocoons and emerge as glowing, gaudy garden tigers. The Captain listened patiently to the last detail of the story of this commonplace miracle, and we gathered that he had come all the way from London to Aviemore neither to fish nor to climb, but as a student of entomology. From him we first learned that this paradise of hills and lochs, woodlands and moors, is endowed with yet another charm.

'Aviemore is a Mecca of the moth men,' the Captain told us. 'Many of us come here from the south for the rare varieties which are found hereabouts.'

Very soon he had the daughters invading his room to see the various families of caterpillars which he had brought with him to feed and tend during his holiday. Again, in the morning, he took the trouble to carry down the Kentish Glory in her glass-windowed prison. Now the scrap of tissue paper which was its only furnishing was dotted with groups of eggs.

'I've counted them. One hundred and fifty-seven,' said the Captain.

'Oh, Daddy, I wish we could catch some moths, and get them to lay, and rear them . . .'

We set off directly after breakfast, up among the birches which, so we had been told, provide the larvae of many species with their food.

'I thought,' I said innocently, 'that moths flew at night. You see them in the glare of the car's headlamps.'

'A lot of types fly by day, too,' the daughters told me authoritatively. 'And even the night-flying kinds can be found, if you know where to look.'

'Where d'you look?'

'On fence posts. On tree-trunks. On stones.'

The Captain had started something. He had been generous with his information. On our journey north we had noticed at one place a rather decrepit fence of railway sleepers. We had talked about it and decided that it must have been erected to keep the snow from drifting on to the line. Now we knew that each year entomologists come from the farthest corners of England just to walk the length of this fence, peering at it and examining it with such minute care that one distinguished member of the fraternity, during the war, was reported as a spy.

On the surface of the sleepers newly hatched moths are wont to rest of a sunny day, drying their wings and preparing for the brief adventure of three-dimensional living.

So, amidst so much fine scenery, we spent a morning and an afternoon inspecting every post of every fence we could discover—and not a moth to be seen. We turned our attention to stones, clambering perilously among the boulders on the steepest part of Craigellachie. No moths, until Sally, leaning into a tiny cave, shouted shrilly:

'I've found one! I've found one!'

We rushed eagerly to the cave, but there was chagrin on Sally's face when we had joined her.

'It's only a dead one, and not even a whole one. Just two pairs of wings.'

And, when we looked again, we saw not merely two pairs but dozens, scattered over the small carpet of moss on the floor of the cave.

In the evening I had a word to say to the Captain, when he had kindly shown the daughters the rarities he had picked up during his day's hunting. I told him about my wild-goose chase, and the excitement which had evaporated when we discovered that all our own captures were as dead as doornails and every one without its body.

I was inviting him to laugh at me, but he did not laugh. He was interested. What was killing the moths? And what moths was it killing? Both points were of as much moment to him as they would have been to me if the wings of dead game birds had been involved. The daughters were asked if they would care to go back to the cave and secure the relics.

Promptly this was done, and up in his room the Captain carefully emptied the tin on to a table and, fitting his monocle, sorted and arranged the collection, never touching them with his fingers, but moving them delicately with forceps. At a glance he could name each species, both in Latin and in English, and there was no question of throwing the scraps of things away. When he returned to

London he took them with him, and the daughters felt justifiably honoured when he sent us a copy of the note he had read about their discovery to no less an august body than the Royal Entomological Society. In it he listed the following separate insects:

1 *Odontosia Carmelita*
1 *Saturnia Pavonia*
15 *Achlya Flavicornis*
1 *Orthosia Gothica*
1 *Orthosia Stabilis*
7 *Orthosia Incerta*
1 *Eupsilia Transversa*
1 *Lycia Hirtaria*

Flavicornis, he reminded the Society, is one of the commonest species at Aviemore in the early spring, with *Incerta* a good second. He concluded:

'No trace of the perpetrator of these foul deeds could be found. A little owl was suspected, but there were no pellets in the cave, and of course a bat may have been the culprit.'

This, by itself, would have been more than enough to delight two youthful and very inexperienced moth-hunters, but it was only a beginning.

Present at the meeting was Professor G. D. Hale Carpenter, president of the Society and head of the Hope Department of Entomology at Oxford University. He had made a request that the collection of wings be passed to him, and presently we were charmed to have a letter from one of his learned assistants, together with a copy of a monograph on *British Insectivorous Bats and their Prey*. The perpetrator of the foul deeds had been positively identified.

'This department,' the letter informed us, 'specializes in bionomic collections, and has very large numbers of these bat rejecta, to which the set you have so kindly sent will make a valuable addition . . .'

'Fame at last!' Sally remarked with a twinkle when we had shared the news.

It would hardly be possible to imagine a less important contribution to a museum than that small handful of insects' wings. Nevertheless, as the discerning reader will have realized, we are a family who do not stint ourselves of the luxury of excitement, even over the most trivial things. We were, and are, absurdly delighted to have caused that microscopic ripple in the pool of Oxford's learning.

Probably the whole art of living happily in the country is based on this capacity to care so much about trifles that there is no sense of loss in letting the bigger things pass. So, ridiculous as it may appear, moths and butterflies came to mean more than mountains on our visit to the Cairngorms.

I have already written something about the joke-makers' traditional cruelty to Aberdonians and to anglers. Their brothers the cartoonists are just as ready to see fair game in the man who goes leaping over the countryside with a net, pursuing butterflies.

Let them laugh! I have been persuaded to do it once or twice. I have suffered all the ludicrous results of being unable to keep my eye on the butterfly and at the same time watch for such hidden snags as roots, boulders, and overgrown ditches. Also, at the end of a hectic chase, my wild swipe usually misses and my insect disappears upwards into the sun. But let me be provocative and assert that it is quite as exhilarating a sport as golf, and not any more incongruous than to go capering across the landscape after a little pill, armed with a handful of sticks!

I am all for the moth-men. The fabric of human knowledge is woven out of many tiny threads, and they are making their contribution. I have come to know a little, but only a very little, about the study of the occurrence of mutations and the slow creation of new varieties. I have been shown similarities between the moths of Scotland and those of Scandinavia and, looking at them, have been told of deductions which set both time and geography in a new perspective. Botany, biology, zoology, ornithology—your moth-hunter is a student of them all, and of much more besides.

The use of it? Mere knowing is its own use. Men's lives can be enriched in many ways which could not be called practical. But those who insist on cash returns and concrete values may well reflect on the possible state of a cultivated and overcrowded earth upon which the insect kingdom was not studied and controlled.

We found that there are as many tricks and stratagems to the tracking down of an entomologist's quarry as there are in the circumventing of an aged and highly educated cock pheasant, and for the enthusiast it has one great advantage over the hunting of feathered game. It is a twenty-four-hour pastime. It can be enjoyed by night as well as by day.

Sometimes we saw the Captain set off with a special lamp fixed to his head. He told us of an exceptionally dark night when the beam of this lamp shone

Moths and butterflies came to mean more than mountains

on a pair of lovers whispering in a gateway. They can have seen only the light, and not the man behind it. They must have thought it was someone carrying an ordinary torch.

'Cor!' said the girl as the Captain passed, 'what a tall man that must be!'

The lure of bright light for the moth tribe is proverbial, and these round-the-clock hunters exploit it by setting up brilliant petrol flares close to sheets coated with a mixture of beer and treacle. Moths come to the glow, and settle to the meal, and are snapped up in the cause of science. But, as a lady in the hotel related, this same magnetism of brightness for night-flying insects can have unexpected results.

It was in Italy. A distinguished company was gathered in a gracious salon, and the talk, which was of art, was erudite and profound. Suddenly an immense, a gigantic moth came fluttering from nowhere and, darting here and there, spread panic. Lofty conversation gave way to squeals of fright. A primitive, unreasoning horror possessed the cultivated minds, but one among the party remained calm enough to plan a way of getting rid of the monster.

'Let's put out the lights,' she said, 'and open the curtains.'

In tense silence the experiment was tried and, true to tradition, the moth flew at once towards the brightest thing that remained. But that was not the window. It was the snowy bosom of a lady in a *décolleté* gown!

And lest I be accused of indulging in cheap laughter at the expense of those frightened people, let me confess that I myself, try as I will, cannot live in any sort of comfort in the presence of a single honey-bee, although my friend John Hankinson keeps seven hives of them buzzing by my garden hedge and I have never once been stung.

The moth-men, we discovered, accept their trophies in all stages from the egg to the ultimate insect. If there are domestic objections to the coating of a sheet with treacle and beer, the same sheet, unsullied, can be spread around the base of some suitable bush or tree. A quick shake of the branches, and down falls a shower of caterpillars which can be reared and transformed into insects all the more perfect for never having roughed it in the world at large.

Many sorts are easily bred in captivity. One collector, while we were at Aviemore, secured a very rare specimen; a moth of an ordinary variety, but with a colour mutation which made it a treasured prize. It was a male. He was proud of it. He was even—for scientists, too, are human—a little boastful about it. He displayed it to his fellows, gently crowing.

He did not enjoy the uniqueness of his trophy for long. The next day another entomologist, in another hotel, captured one with the same oddity of colouring —and a female at that. If it laid, this rival might have dozens of the rarity.

There were two or three days of tension, and then a gradual easing of the strain. No news arrived of any eggs. The daughters, whose partisanship had been quite uninhibited, seemed somehow disappointed at so flat an ending to so exciting a situation.

'Couldn't the two be mated?' Sally suggested.

Forthwith, a marriage was arranged. The two unique moths were introduced, and within a few hours there were eggs in plenty. These were scrupulously counted and fairly divided, and carried away to be hatched and tended.

The men who were so generous in sharing with us the thrills of their fascinating hobby were amateurs in the highest sense, and not interested in the commercial side of it. They were modest in their demands upon the local insect population, taking only what they required for their private use. They deplored the existence of certain others who had no scruples about denuding an area of some rare type, merely for money.

It can be real money. We heard of a man who in next to no time earned himself a thousand pounds by breeding and selling curiously marked specimens of the ordinary currant moth.

The name of the collector who bought them happened to be Rothschild.

The Captain departed, well satisfied with his trip, but his passage across our lives had left a permanent impression.

May brought warmer weather. Butterflies hatched—fritillaries, orange-tips, and also countless moths which were to be seen dancing and flirting on the moors in the sunshine. We found ourselves taking a surprising amount of pleasure in the existence of something which had been under our noses all our lives without ever having been noticed.

A new guest arrived at the hotel, a tall, lean, studious-looking man who approached Sally after dinner.

'Are you Miss Young—the lady who found the moth wings in the cave?'

For once the elder daughter was almost wordless, in awe of her own renown. The stranger mentioned that he had heard of the discovery in London. He wished to be escorted to the bat's dining-room, and very soon, gathering still more wings, he was reading a potted record of the types which were flying on Speyside at that period of the year.

He was Baron de Worms, friend of Captain Jackson, R.N., and it was these two who, by opening our eyes to the delights of a new and fascinating pastime, spared us the effort of climbing to the high tops for holiday adventures, and instead put excitement into every shrub and tussock around Aviemore.

From Baron de Worms we learned the art of softening specimens in the relaxing tin, and then of fixing them down with strips of cellophane and a multiplicity of pins on a cork-topped setting-board, with careful attention to the placing of wings, legs, and feelers, so that when they had rested and stiffened there for a week or two they could be lifted off and tucked away in some box, their beauty perfectly displayed.

Our last day at Aviemore was the warmest and sunniest of all. I had a half-hearted hankering for climbing just one Cairngorm before we departed, but I left the choice of the final adventure to the family.

'Let's go to Glen Gurgle,' they said.

This name will not be found on any map, nor would the glen's contours make the slightest impression on one with a scale of anything less than six inches to the mile.

It is a specific place, and yet there are hundreds of it scattered over Scotland. We christened it for ourselves, in honour of the tiny stream which tumbles musically down its brief length in a series of miniature Niagaras. Pine trees and birch trees and dark clumps of juniper are dotted about the heather which clothes its fairyland slopes. Great bunches of long-stalked primroses grow in the shady places, and the song of the water is a joy.

We liked the Spey. We loved the boisterous Druie enough to set out early one morning and follow its main arm, the Allt na Beinne Mor, all the way to its source in Loch Einich—and there, as a reward for our pains, we saw a herd of red deer go splashing across the burn and away up the hillside. We could not look at the outlines of the Cairngorms or the Grampians without feeling uplifted. But our favourite spot of all was Glen Gurgle.

Thither we cycled for a final farewell, and we had hardly arrived when another cyclist rode up and dismounted with a friendly 'Ah!', and we had the best of possible company.

Baron de Worms had brought two butterfly nets, and it was not only the daughters who were eager to use the spare one.

We climbed higher, away from the trees, and we started looking at stones. The moorland was dotted with great grey boulders; ordinary, dead lumps of rock. Baron de Worms signalled us to one, and pointed.

'D'you see it?'

We saw only a stone.

'A knot-grass moth,' he said, and one granule of the rock became, when he had all but put a finger on it, a bit of life so perfectly camouflaged that we might have passed a thousand and noticed none. It was newly emerged, and still quite helpless, sitting there invisible in the full glare of the sun while its wings dried and gathered the power of flight.

So, amid all the glories of the Highlands, we spent what is still remembered as a perfect afternoon methodically quartering one small patch in that stretch of moorland—gazing at boulders. We each found one knot-grass moth. Just one apiece, and only a moth. But still, in some curious way, that day must be written down as a day of rare delight.

We returned to our own countryside, our many pets, our garden, our familiar horizon. We exclaimed, as one always must, at the commonplace and yet miraculous changes which a few weeks of spring had wrought. It had been good to be away; it was, somehow, still better to be back.

Soon—and how welcome!—there were knockings at our door. Friend Edna, to rush Margie off to inspect a new puppy; friend Marjorie, with an account of new livestock at Flatfield Farm and an urgent invitation; adult friends of my own and my wife's to complete the sense of being home. A poor affair it would be without someone, occasionally, at the door.

'Living in a place like this,' one visitor told us, 'you don't need to go on holiday.'

A dangerous thought! We like our corner of Strathmore so much that we go away too seldom. Sweet as any place may be, it would surely be a disaster to lose entirely that sense of something wonderful lying on the other side of the hills. However delightful, a house in the country should not be allowed to become a prison.

At dusk on our first evening at home we went out with a torch, and there, flying everywhere, were moths. We had not noticed them before. We came in, and they were fluttering against the windows, caught by the light. We saw them.

This seeing is everything. It is probably of importance to the townsman too, but it is vital to the countryman, who finds the world either empty or teeming according to how much he notices.

A short time after we got back I met on the road an old tinker who was carrying under his arm a bundle of fine, straight ash sticks. He offered a passing greeting, as tinkers usually will, and I stopped for a chat.

'What,' I asked him, 'is the best time of year to cut a walking-stick?'
His gnarled face crinkled in a wise, old-fashioned grin.
'The best time,' he said, 'is to cut it as soon as you spot it.'
'And where's the likeliest sort of place to get good ones?'
'Where you look hardest!'
There is no deeper secret to the finding of any of the other treasures or pleasures of country living.